GRAMMAR DNA

GRAMMAR DNA

영어 문장 분석의
새로운 패러다임

조 기 석

HUiNE

Preface

Grammar DNA

대한민국의 문법 교육은 오랫동안 동사위주로 문장을 분석해왔다. 본 교재 Grammar DNA는 동사위주의 문장 분석에서 벗어나 술어위주로 문장을 분석하는 새로운 문법 패러다임을 제시한다. 동사위주로 문장을 분석할 경우 5형식의 틀에 한정되기 쉬우며 동사의 품사가 변화되면 의미가 같은 두 문장을 전혀 다른 유형의 문장으로 분석하게 된다. 하지만 술어 위주의 문장 분석에서는 동사의 품사변화에 상관없이 일관성 있는 의미위주의 문장 분석이 가능하다. 본 교재 Grammar DNA는 술어위주의 문장 분석을 통해서 영어 구문 분석에 대한 새로운 시각을 제시하고 술어위주의 문법교육을 널리 보급하기 위한 목적으로 집필되었다. 본 교재가 대한민국의 영어교육에 있어서 새로운 장르를 펼칠 수 있는 계기가 되기를 바란다.

끝으로 본 교재가 나올 수 있도록 많은 격려와 도움을 주신 성은경 교수님, 김희진 교수님, 이선영 교수님, 윤도현 교수님, 이기택 교수님, 임익희 교수님, 조은형 교수님, 김지인 교수님, 김귀원 교수님, 정철원 선생님, 남태경 선생님, 강연지 선생님, 장윤정 선생님, 박선영 선생님, 임진태 선생님, 이민욱 선생님, 이보름 선생님, 이정애 선생님, 그리고 출판부 신선호 과장님께 감사의 마음을 전하며, 부족한 나를 오늘날까지 인도하신 하나님께 이 저서를 바친다.

2013년 9월

저자 조기석

Contents

Grammar DNA

UNIT 1

문장의 기본구조

Basic Sentence Structure

Warm Up

Basic Sentence Structure

Comp	Subject	Tense	Neg	Link	Aspect	Predicate

- Comp(보문어) : 문장의 유형을 나타내는 요소, 주절과 종속절을 연결하는 문장접속사
- Subject(주어) : 술어와 유기적인 의미관계를 갖는 요소
- Tense(시제) : 문장의 시제(과거, 현재, 미래)를 나타내는 요소
- Neg(부정어) : 문장을 부정문으로 만드는 요소
- Link(연결어) : 두 문장 성분의 연결을 가능하게 하는 요소
- Aspect(상) : 진행이나 완료를 나타내는 요소
- Predicate(술어) : 의미상의 주어를 취하는 요소

Qviz 1

다음 보기에 주어진 예문을 잘 살펴보고 물음에 답하시오.

Ex

1. She is clearing the snow.
2. He has just arrived.
3. Sue was punished.
4. Maureen will inherit her father's business.
5. Kerry does not have a smartphone yet.
6. Jina is very disappointed.

1. 위 문장에서 붉은색 동사의 공통적인 역할은 무엇인가?

① 시제(tcnsc) ② 진행(progressive aspect)
③ 완료(perfect aspect) ④ 술어(predicate)

2. 위 문장에서 푸른 색 단어의 공통적인 역할은 무엇인가?

① 시제(tense) ② 진행(progressive aspect)
③ 완료(perfective aspect) ④ 술어(predicate)

술어 : 의미상의 주어를 취하는 요소

Quiz 2

다음 보기에 주어진 예문을 잘 살펴보고 물음에 답하시오.

Ex

1. a. She is clearing the snow.
   b. She will still be clearing the snow tomorrow.
2. a. He has not just arrived.
   b. He will have arrived by then.
3. a. The project is still underway.
   b. It should be finished soon.

1. 위 문장에서 붉은색 동사는 시제를 나타내며 파란색 동사는 의미상의 주어를 취하는 술어 역할을 하고 있다. 그렇다면 보라색 동사의 역할은 무엇인가?

____.

Quiz 3

다음 보기에 주어진 예문을 잘 살펴보고 물음에 답하시오.

Ex

1. a. She is usually not kind to her brothers.
   b. She is being kind to her sisters now.
   c. She will not be kind to her parents.
   d. She will not be being kind to her children.
2. a. He has been exercising for a long time.
   b. The exercycle will have been used for a long time.

1. (1b)와 (1d) 문장에서 파란색 동사의 역할은 무엇인가?

① 시제(tense) ② 진행(progressive aspect)
③ 완료(perfective aspect) ④ 술어(predicate)

2. (2a)와 (2b) 문장에서 파란색 동사의 역할은 무엇인가?

① 시제(tense) ② 진행(progressive aspect)
③ 완료(perfective aspect) ④ 술어(predicate)

Lecture 1

Sentence Analysis

Definition of Seven Basic Sentence Elements

Comp	Subject	Tense	Neg	Link	Aspect	Predicate

- Comp(보문어) : 문장의 유형을 나타내는 요소, 주절과 종속절을 연결하는 문장접속사
- Subject(주어) : 술어와 유기적인 의미관계를 갖는 요소
- Tense(시제) : 문장의 시제(과거, 현재, 미래)를 나타내는 요소
- Neg(부정어) : 문장을 부정문으로 만드는 요소
- Link(연결어) : 두 문장 성분의 연결을 가능하게 하는 요소
- Aspect(상) : 진행이나 완료를 나타내는 요소
- Predicate(술어) : 의미상의 주어를 취하는 요소

Sentence Analysis

(1)

The computer	does	not	work	at all.
Subj	Tense	Neg	Pred	Mod

(2)

The engineer	was	called.
Subj	Tense	Pred

(3)

He	has	arrived.
Subj	Tense	Pred

(4)

He	is	not	serious.
Subj	Tense	Neg	Pred

(5)

We	are	disappointed.
Subj	Tense	Pred

(6)

The repair job	is	not	going well.
Subj	Tense	Neg	Pred

(7)

He	is	not	being	handy.
Subj	Tense	Neg	Aspect	Pred

(8)

The computer	will	not	be	repaired.
Subj	Tense	Neg	Link	Pred

(9)

The repair job	will	not	have	been	completed	by late evening.
Subj	Tense	Neg	Link	Aspect	Pred	Mod

(10)

We	are	being	annoyed.
Subj	Tense	Aspect	Pred

(11)

His colleague	has	arrived.
Subj	Tense	Pred

(12)

He	is	very handy.
Subj	Tense	Pred

(13)

How well	the computer	works	again!
Comp	Subj	Pred	Mod

Special Tips on Predicates and Tense 1

- Predicates are essential elements to form sentences. The predicates almost always have a subject and determine the number and types of sentence elements. Even a simple sentence like "(Be) quiet" has a predicate.

Ex	Quiet.
	Predicate

- The categories of the predicates vary from verbs, adjectives, progressive participles, perfect participles, and passive participles.

(1) Verbs

Ex	He	smiles.
	Subj	Predicate

(2) Adjectives

Ex	She	is	angry.
	Subj	Tense	Predicate

(3) Progressive participles

Ex	He	is	sleeping.
	Subj	Tense	Predicate

(4) Perfect participles

Ex	She	has	woken up.
	Subj	Tense	Predicate

(5) Passive participles

Ex	He	was	scolded.
	Subj	Tense	Predicate

- Tense is a sentence element that determines the tense of sentences. The types of tense are past, present, and future. Sometimes the tense appears on the predicate, but basically the tense and predicate are separate. Even when the predicate is deleted, the tense is not deleted but remains to specify the tense of the sentence.

Ex

Judy: Hey! I hear that you went on a blind date yesterday. Did it go well?

Sue: Yes, it was fabulous. I like him a lot. I'm so lucky to have met him!

Judy: What's the guy like? Is he handsome?

Sue: No, he isn't [ ]. He is rather plain.

Judy: Is he smart? I bet he's really interesting to talk to; right?

Sue: No, he isn't [ ]. He is pretty boring. I'd rather watch paint dry than have a conversation with him.

Judy: Can he drive?

Sue: No, he can't [ ]. He has a driver's licence, and even though he's got a nice car, he never actually learned how to drive.

Judy: Does he smoke?

Sue: Yes, he does [ ]. He is a heavy smoker.

Judy: Well, then how come you like him?

Sue: He is fantastically wealthy.

Judy: Oh, he is [ ]? I see.

Dialogue 1

Lauren: Glenn, didn't you hear the news? Haven't you heard?

Glenn: No, I haven't [ ]. What are you talking about?

Lauren: Smoking is outlawed here.

Glenn: Smoking? Outlawed? That's impossible. Says who?

Lauren: Say's the law. It changed last week.

Glenn: Laws don't just change.

Lauren: Looks like they do [ ] to me.

Glenn: Unbelievable. I have to smoke.

Lauren: That's nonsense. Nobody has to [ ]. You're just saying that because you're addicted.

Glenn: No, I'm not [ ]

Lauren: Aren't you afraid that you will be fined?

Glenn: I don't think I'll be [ ]. That law is so ridiculous, Lauren. It's only meant to scare tourists. Smoking is a part of who we are as a people. I see my cigarettes as a cultural necessity, a real cultural accessory.

Lauren: Ok, now I think you are ridiculous.

Glenn: No, I'm not [ ].

Lauren: Well, the government is changing the law so suddenly, but the law is the law. Besides, outlawing smoking may be detrimental to the economy, but allowing smoking is detrimental to your health.

Glenn: Gee.

Q. 위 대화문에서 생략된 단어들의 공통적인 문장성분은 무엇인가?

① Comp ② Tense ③ Aspect ④ Predicate

정답 : ④

Exercise 1

1. 다음 주어진 문장성분들을 순서대로 배열하시오.

Tense / Subject / Neg / Link / Aspect

Comp ①______ ②______ ③______ ④______ ⑤______ Predicate

2. 다음 문제를 풀어보세요.

(1) 의미상의 주어를 취하면서 문장을 형성하는 데 가장 필수적인 요소는?

① Tense ② Neg ③ Link ④ Aspect ⑤ Predicate

(2) 진행이나 완료를 나타내는 문장성분은?

① Tense ② Neg ③ Link ④ Aspect ⑤ Predicate

(3) 부정문을 만드는 문장성분은?

① Tense ② Neg ③ Link ④ Aspect ⑤ Predicate

(4) 두 문장 성분의 연결기능을 하는 문장성분은?

① Tense ② Neg ③ Link ④ Aspect ⑤ Predicate

3. 다음 보기에 주어진 예문에서 붉은 색 단어들의 공통적인 역할은 무엇인가?

Ex

1. a. Bill is surprised that his son won the top prize at the contest.
   b. His wife will be also surprised.
2. a. Kerry is being kind to his mother.
   b. His wife will be being kind to her as well.
3. a. Cathy has not finished the project yet.
   b. She will not have finished the project by the end of this month, either.
4. a. Mr. Kim has not returned home yet.
   b. He will not have returned home by midnight, either.

① Tense(시제)　② Link(연결어)　③ Aspect(상)　④ Predicate(술어)

4. 다음 보기에 주어진 예문에서 붉은 색 단어들의 공통적인 역할은 무엇인가?

Ex

1. a. John has studied English for five years.
   b. His son has been studying English for more than five years.
2. a. The beggar has touched the lady for a dime.
   b. The lady has been touched for a dime.
3. a. Mary is usually kind to senior citizens.
   b. Her daughter is being kind to some senior citizens.
4. a. The tall guy is talking to the attractive girl.
   b. The attractive girl is being talked to by the tall guy.

① Tense(시제)　② Link(연결어)　③ Aspect(상)　④ Predicate(술어)

5. 밑줄 친 단어의 문장성분을 보기에서 찾아 결정해보세요.

Comp	Subject	Tense	Neg	Link	Aspect	Predicate	Modifier

(1) Judy is fit.

(2) She is not fat.

(3) Timothy is gloomy.

(4) He will not be happy.

(5) Tony does not exercise.

(6) He must be overweight.

(7) The new building has not been constructed yet.

(8) The construction will not have been completed by the end of this year.

6. 다음 주어진 예문을 잘 살펴보고 물음에 답하시오.

Ex

1. Mr. Smith is underweight.
2. Mrs. Smith is matronly.
3. Jack was punished.
4. Jill was praised.
5. Jim has not come back home.
6. His wife and children have returned home.
7. The boy does not exercise.
8. The girl does not drive.
9. The man is not smoking.
10. The woman is not drinking.

(1) 위 예문에서 시제를 나타내기 위해서 다른 조동사가 사용되고 있다. 술어가 형용사일 때 사용되는 시제동사는 무엇인가?

① be 동사 ② have 동사 ③ do 동사 ④ 서법조동사

(2) 술어가 수동형 분사(passive participle)일 때 사용되는 시제동사는 무엇인가?

① be 동사 ② have 동사 ③ do 동사 ④ 서법조동사

(3) 술어가 완료형 분사(perfect participle)일 때 사용되는 시제동사는 무엇인가?

① be 동사 ② have 동사 ③ do 동사 ④ 서법조동사

(4) 술어가 진행형 분사(progressive participle)일 때 사용되는 시제동사는 무엇인가?

① be 동사 ② have 동사 ③ do 동사 ④ 서법조동사

(5) 술어가 일반동사(동사원형)일 때 사용되는 시제동사는 무엇인가?

① be 동사 ② have 동사 ③ do 동사 ④ 서법조동사

Coffee Break

성(family name)의 기원

우리 한국인에게 이름 외에 성(family name)이 있는 것처럼 영 미인에게도 성이 있습니다. 우리 한국인의 성은 대부분 조상들의 출신지역을 의미합니다. 한국인들의 성 중에서 김씨, 이씨, 그리고 박씨가 대표적인 성이라고 할 수 있습니다. 이러한 성들은 최초의 조상들이 살았던 지역을 의미합니다. 김해 김씨, 전주 이씨, 그리고 밀양 박씨와 같은 예를 보면 성씨가 출신지역을 의미한다는 것을 잘 알 수 있습니다.

영 미인들의 성은 우리와는 다르게 여러 가지 기원에서 시작되었습니다. 그 중에 하나가 직업(occupation)입니다. Mr. Smith라는 성은 대장장이를 뜻하는 blacksmith에서 왔고, Mr. Baker라는 성은 빵을 굽는 제빵업자 baker에서 유래되었습니다. Mr. Carpenter는 목수를 뜻하는 carpenter에서 왔으며 Mr. Taylor는 재단사 tailor에서 시작되었습니다.

Quiz. 그렇다면 Mr. Miller의 Miller는 어떤 직업에서 유래되었을까요?

① 물레 방앗간 주인 ② 호프집 주인 ③ 등대지기 ④ 밀 판매업자

정답 : ①

Lecture 2

Basic Sentence Structure

Comp	Subj	Tense	Neg	Link	Aspect	Predicate

Sentence Analysis

Example 1 The musical is popular.

Stage 1

Comp	Subject	Tense	Neg	Link	Aspect	Predicate
						popular

Stage 2

Comp	Subject	Tense	Neg	Link	Aspect	Predicate
	The musical	is				popular

Example 2 The opera will not be so popular.

Stage 1

Comp	Subject	Tense	Neg	Link	Aspect	Predicate
						so popular

Stage 2

Comp	Subject	Tense	Neg	Link	Aspect	Predicate
	The opera	will	not	be		so popular

Example 3

Is she being kind to the senior citizen?

Stage	Comp	Subject	Tense	Neg	Link	Aspect	Predicate	Object
Stage 1							kind	
Stage 2		she	is			being	kind	
Stage 3		she	is			being	kind	to the senior citizen
Stage 4	Is	she				being	kind	to the senior citizen

Example 4

A delegation has not returned.

Stage	Comp	Subject	Tense	Neg	Link	Aspect	Predicate
Stage 1							returned
Stage 2		A delegation	has	not			returned

Example 5 The delegation will not have returned by the end of this week.

Stage 1

Comp	Subject	Tense	Neg	Link	Aspect	Predicate	Mod
						returned	

Stage 2

Comp	Subject	Tense	Neg	Link	Aspect	Predicate	Mod
	The delegation	will	not	have		returned	

Stage 3

Comp	Subject	Tense	Neg	Link	Aspect	Predicate	Mod
	The delegation	will	not	have		returned	by the end of this week

Example 6 The essay was not written yet.

Stage 1

Comp	Subject	Tense	Neg	Link	Aspect	Predicate	Mod
						written	

Stage 2

Comp	Subject	Tense	Neg	Link	Aspect	Predicate	Mod
	The essay	was	not			written	

Stage 3

Comp	Subject	Tense	Neg	Link	Aspect	Predicate	Mod
	The essay	was	not			written	yet

Example 7 — When will the essay have been written?

	Comp	Subject	Tense	Neg	Link	Aspect	Predicate	Mod
Stage 1							written	
Stage 2		the essay	will		have	been	written	when
Stage 3	When will	the essay			have	been	written	

Example 8 — Didn't Benita smile yesterday?

	Comp	Subject	Tense	Neg	Link	Aspect	Predicate	Mod
Stage 1							smile	
Stage 2		Benita	did	not			smile	yesterday
Stage 3		Benita	didn't				smile	yesterday
Stage 4	Didn't	Benita					smile	yesterday

Example 9 Harry did smile the day before yesterday.

	Comp	Subject	Tense	Neg	Link	Aspect	Predicate	Mod
Stage 1							**smile**	
Stage 2		**Harry**	**did**				**smile**	**the day before yesterday**
Stage 3		**Harry**					**smiled**	**the day before yesterday**

Special Tips on Predicates and Tense 2

- The Predicates determine the number and type of sentence elements. The Tense determines the tense of the sentence. The Tense and the Predicate are basically separate, but sometimes the Tense and the Predicate are fused into one.

1. a. He did not die in his early seventies.
   b. He *did* die in his late seventies.
   c. He died in his late seventies.
   d. She was not dead in her early eighties.
   e. She was dead in her late eighties.

2. a. She did not hesitate at first.
   b. She *did* hesitate in the end.
   c. She hesitated in the end.
   d. She was not hesitant to get married.
   e. She was hesitant to get divorced.

3. a. He did not succeed in the beginning of his life.
   b. He *did* succeed at the end of his life.
   c. He succeeded at the end of his life.
   d. She was not successful at the beginning of her career.
   e. She was successful at the end of her career.

4. a. The democrat does not rely on military power.
   b. The democrat *does* rely on justice.
   c. The democrat relies on justice.
   d. The dictator is not reliant on justice.
   e. The dictator is reliant on military power.

Dialogue 2

Liz: Oh, Brain! Isn't it terrible about Amy and Jake?

Brian: Did something happen?

Liz: Haven't you heard? They got a divorce. Divorce is so awful. Twenty six years is a long time, but Amy said she's fine. She told Elaine that she's fine.

Brian: Are you serious?

Liz: Yes. Amy has been wanting a divorce for 3 years.

Brian: Has she really? Am I that out of the loop?

Liz: I can't believe you didn't know about it.

Brian: I just can't believe it. Could you imagine trying to navigate the dating scene after so long? This news is such a shock to me. I have never been so surprised in my life.

Liz: Yes, you have. Do you remember when she quit her job at the gallery for him? Now that was a shock!

Brian: Well, did she have a prenup with Jake? Will they go to court over the estate?

Liz: I don't know. Time will tell. You seem to have gotten over the shock pretty quick. Were you expecting it?

Brian: The timing seems strange. I wonder why she'd bother to break up after so many years. But I've always thought that Jake was a bad husband. Maybe it's for the best.

Liz: Can it be a sign of the times? I don't know. Maybe.

Q. 위 대화문에서 의문문을 형성하기 위해 Comp 자리로 이동하는 단어들은 무엇인가? (둘을 고르시오.)

① 시제동사 ② 진행동사 ③ 부정어 ④ 의문사

정답: ①, ④

Exercise 1

Ex

1. a. He did not die in his early seventies.
   b. He *did* die in his late seventies.
   c. He died in his late seventies.
   d. She was not dead in her early eighties.
   e. She was dead in her late eighties.

1. 위 예문에서 시제와 술어가 하나로 융합되어 있는 경우는 어느 것인가?

① a　　② b　　③ c　　④ d　　⑤ e

2. 위 예문에서 붉은색 단어들의 공통적인 문장성분은 무엇인가?

① 시제(tense)　　② 진행(progressive aspect)

③ 완료(perfective aspect)　　④ 술어(predicate)

3. 위 예문에서 (a), (b), (c)번 문장들의 술어와 (d)번과 (e)번 문장들의 술어는 서로 어떠한 차이가 있나?

① 시제(tense)의 차이　　② 상(aspect)의 차이　　③ 의미의 차이　　④ 품사의 차이

4. 다음 보기에 주어진 예문을 살펴보고 물음에 답하시오.

Ex

1. a. He is upset.
   b. Is he upset?
2. a. She has come back home.
   b. Has she come back home?
3. a. The train had already left when he got to the station.
   b. Had the train already left when he got to the station?
4. a. The new camera does not work.
   b. Does the new camera not work?

위 보기에 주어진 예문들은 평서문에서 의문이 형성되는 과정을 보여주고 있다. 의문문 형성을 위해서 Comp 자리로 이동하는 붉은색 동사들의 공통점은 무엇인가?

① 시제(tense)　　② 진행(progressive aspect)

③ 완료(perfect aspect)　　④ 술어(predicate)

5. 다음 문장에서 언더라인 된 단어들의 문장성분을 보기에서 결정하시오.

Ex　Comp　Subject　Tense　Neg　Link　Aspect　Predicate　Modifier

(1) The comedy was really exciting.

(2) Was the tragedy equally exciting?

(3) The man is not kind at all.

(4) Is he being kind temporarily?

(5) The project has not been finished yet.

(6) When will the project have been completed?

(7) Marina didn't smile.

(8) Didn't her husband smile either?

6. 다음 주어진 문장을 잘 살펴보고 물음에 답하시오.

Ex Comp Subject Tense Neg Link Aspect Predicate

1. a. The boy will not often be scolded.
   b. He will not often be praised, either.
2. a. Sue has not always been kind to her friends.
   b. She has occasionally been good to some of her friends.
3. a. I can hardly ask my parents for money.
   b. My parents barely make enough money to pay their bills.
4. a. John has never seen his parents.
   b. He had barely arrived home before his parents left.
5. a. Jina is always complaining to her boss.
   b. She is always bothering him.
6. a. Harry seldom goes to church.
   b. He hardly ever goes out on Sundays.
7. a. Jina is often late to school.
   b. She never arrives on time.

위 예문에서 문장 내에서 빈도분사의 위치를 모두 통합적으로 설명하기 위해서 빈도부사(frequency adverb)의 위치를 어디에 설정해야하나?

____.

Wrap Up

Basic Sentence Structure

Comp Subject Tense Neg Link Aspect Predicate

- Comp(보문어) : 문장의 유형을 나타내는 요소, 주절과 종속절을 연결하는 문장접속사
- Subject(주어) : 술어와 유기적인 의미적 관계를 갖는 요소
- Tense(시제) : 문장의 시제(과거, 현재, 미래)를 나타내는 요소
- Neg(부정어) : 문장을 부정문으로 만드는 요소
- Link(연결어) : 두 문장성분의 연결을 가능하게 하는 요소
- Aspect(상) : 진행이나 완료를 나타내는 요소
- Predicate(술어) : 의미상의 주어를 취하는 요소

UNIT 2 1가 술어에 대한 이해

One-Place Predicate Sentences

Warm Up

술어(predicate)는 문장을 형성하는 데 가장 핵심이 되는 요소로서 기본적으로 의미상의 주어를 취하는 요소입니다. 술어는 다음과 같이 크게 3가지 유형으로 분류할 수 있습니다.

1. 1가 술어 (one-place predicate)
2. 2가 술어 (two-place predicate)
3. 3가 술어 (three-place predicate)

- 1가 술어(one-place predicate)는 주어(subject)나 명제(proposition)와 같은 하나의 문장성분을 가지고 문장을 형성할 수 있는 술어입니다.

- 2가 술어(two-place predicate)는 문장을 형성하기 위해서 주어 외에 또 하나의 문장성분을 필요로 하는 술어로서 주어를 포함해서 두 개의 문장성분을 가지고 문장을 형성하는 술어입니다.

- 3가 술어는 주어를 포함해서 총 세 개의 문장성분으로 문장을 형성하는 술어입니다. 술어가 1가 술어인지, 2가 술어인지 아니면 3가 술어인지는 문장에서 술어가 몇 개의 문장성분을 필요로 하는 지를 기준으로 판단할 수 있습니다.

Qviz 1

다음 보기에 주어진 예문을 잘 살펴보고 물음에 답하시오.

Ex

1. Kerry is sick.
2. His wife is worried.
3. A doctor was called.
4. He has arrived.
5. The liquid medicine does not work.
6. The powdered medicine works wonders.
7. His fever has broken.
8. His wife is happy.
9. They are smiling.

1. 위 문장에서 파란색 단어의 공통점은 무엇인가?

① 동사(verb)　② 형용사(adjective)　③ 1가 술어　④ 2가 술어

1가 술어 : 주어만을 가지고 문장을 형성할 수 있는 술어
2가 술어 : 주어 외에 또 하나의 문장 성분이 필요한 술어

2. 위 보기에 주어진 문장 1~9에서 시제와 술어가 하나로 융합된 문장은 어떤 문장인가?

① 6번 문장　② 7번 문장　③ 8번 문장　④ 9번 문장

Quiz 2

다음 보기에 주어진 예문을 잘 살펴보고 물음에 답하시오.

Ex

1. Lydia has a boyfriend.
2. His name is Tony Wilson.
3. He will make a good husband.
4. She asked her parents' permission to marry him.
5. Her parents consented to their marriage.
6. He is delighted at the news.
7. Their wedding took place in a luxurious, fancy hotel.
8. The newlyweds are leaving for Paris for their honeymoon.
9. They have just come back from their honeymoon in Paris.
10. Their suitcase is full of gifts.

1. 위 보기에 주어진 문장에서 파란색 단어의 공통점은 무엇인가?

① 동사(verb) ② 형용사(adjective) ③ 1가 술어 ④ 2가 술어

2. 세 번째 문장 "He will make a good husband."에서 'make'의 의미는?

① ~을 만들다 ② ~이 되다 ③ ~ 이다 ④ ~이 있다

Quiz 3

다음 보기에 주어진 예문을 잘 살펴보고 물음에 답하시오.

Ex

1. The boss informed his foreign employees of the new regulation.
2. The new regulation keeps the foreign employees from smoking in the office.
3. The foreign employees asked the boss to explain the new regulation in English.
4. The boss cannot make himself understood in English.
5. The boss did not even post an English version of the regulation on the board.
6. The employees blamed him for his negligence.
7. They even filled the company's homepage with complaints.
8. The boss finally announced to his foreign employees that the new regulation had been cancelled.

1\. 위 보기에 주어진 문장에서 파란색 단어의 공통점은 무엇인가?

① 1가 술어 ② 2가 술어 ③ 3가 술어 ④ 자동사

2\. 사장님이 제시한 새로운 규칙의 내용은 무엇인가?

① 한국인 직원들이 사무실에서 담배를 피울 수 없다.

② 한국인 직원들이 사무실 밖에서 담배를 피울 수 없다.

③ 외국인 직원들이 사무실에서 담배를 피울 수 없다.

④ 외국인 직원들이 사무실 밖에서 담배를 피울 수 없다.

Lecture 1 One-Place Predicate with Subject

Basic Sentence Structure

Comp　Subject　Tense　Neg　Link　Aspect　Predicate

- Comp(보문어) : 문장의 유형을 나타내는 요소, 주절과 종속절을 연결하는 문장접속사
- Subj(주어) : 술어와 유기적인 의미적 관계를 갖는 요소
- Tense(시제) : 문장의 시제(과거, 현재, 미래)를 나타내는 요소
- Neg(부정어) : 문장을 부정문으로 만드는 요소
- Link(연결어) : 두 문장 성분의 연결을 가능하게 하는 요소
- Aspect(상) : 진행이나 완료를 나타내는 요소
- Predicate(술어) : 의미상의 주어를 취하며 문장성분의 수와 종류를 결정하는 요소
  - 1가 술어 : 하나의 문장성분으로 문장을 형성할 수 있는 술어
  - 2가 술어 : 두 개의 문장성분으로 문장을 형성할 수 있는 술어
  - 3가 술어 : 세 개의 문장성분으로 문장을 형성할 수 있는 술어

1. A Paradigm of English Grammar

- One-Place Predicate Sentences

  a. Comp + Subj + Tense + Neg + Predicate-1

  b. Comp + Expl + Tense + Neg + Predicate-1 + Proposition

- Two-Place Predicate Sentences

  a. Comp + Subj + Tense + Neg + Predicate-2 + SC

  b. Comp + Subj + Tense + Neg + Predicate-2 + Obj

  c. Comp + Subj + Tense + Neg + Predicate-2 + Cause

d. Comp + Subj + Tense + Neg + Predicate-2 + Loc

e. Comp + Subj + Tense + Neg + Predicate-2 + Goal

f. Comp + Subj + Tense + Neg + Predicate-2 + Source

g. Comp + Subj + Tense + Neg + Predicate-2 + Substance

- Three-Place Predicate Sentences

a. Comp + Subj + Tense + Neg + Predicate-3 + Do + IO

b. Comp + Subj + Tense + Neg + Predicate-3 + IO + DO

c. Comp + Subj + Tense + Neg + Predicate-3 + Obj + Obiect Complement

d. Comp + Subj + Tense + Neg + Predicate-3 + Obj + Loc

e. Comp + Subj + Tense + Neg + Predicate-3 + Obj + Cause

f. Comp + Subj + Tense + Neg + Predicate-3 + Obj + Substance

2. One-Place Predicate Sentences

- Comp + Subj + Tense + Neg + Predicate-1
- Comp + Expl + Tense + Neg + Predicate-1 + Proposition
  - 1가 술어 : 하나의 문장성분을 가지고 문장을 형성할 수 있는 술어
  - 주어:
    - 술어와 유기적인 의미적 관계를 갖는 요소
    - 술어 앞에 위치함
    - 명사(구) 또는 절로 되어 있음
  - 명제:
    - 술어와 유기적인 의미적 관계를 갖는 요소
    - 술어 뒤에 위치함
    - 절로 되어 있음
    - 종속절의 주어가 주절의 주어로 이동할 수 있음

Sentence Analysis

Comp Subject Tense Neg Link Aspect Predicate-1

(1) Jane	worked	very hard.
Subj	Pred-1	Mod

(2) Bill	was	not	hard-working.
Subj	Tense	Neg	Pred-1

(3) She	did	not	hesitate	at the critical moment in her life.
Subj	Tense	Neg	Pred-1	Mod

(4) He	was	hesitant	at every critical moment in his life.
Subj	Tense	Pred-1	Mod

(5) She	made a decision	very quickly.
Subj	Pred-1	Mod

(6) He	was	not	decisive	at all.
Subj	Tense	Neg	Pred-1	Mod

(7) She	succeeded	in the end.
Subj	Pred-1	Mod

(8) He	was	hardly	successful.
Subj	Tense	Mod	Pred-1

(9) She	finally	died	in her late eighties.
Subj	Mod	Pred-1	Mod

(10) He	was	finally	dead	in his early sixties.
Subj	Tense	Mod	Pred-1	Mod

Special Tips on Predicates and Tense 1

- Types of predicates

Predicates are essential elements in the formation of sentences. There are three types of predicates: **one-place predicates**, **two-place predicates**, and **three-place predicates**. **One-place predicates** must have **one syntactic element** such as **a subject** or **proposition**. **Two-place predicates** must have one more syntactic element in addition to the subject, such as **a subject complement**, **object**, **cause**, **location**, **goal**, **source**, or **substance**. **Three-place predicates** must have two more syntactic elements in addition to the subject, such as **a direct object followed by an indirect object**, **an indirect object followed by a direct object**, **an object plus an object complement**, **an object plus a location**, or **an object plus a substance**. The pattern of sentences varies depending on the types of predicates. Therefore when analyzing sentences, we need to check what types of predicates the sentences have.

Dialogue 1

Jack: What did you do this weekend?

Megan: I went skydiving with Paul and Mei!

Jack: Wow, that sounds exciting? How was it?

Megan: Well, it was a spur of a moment decision. Paul hesitated at first.

Jack: Paul was hesitant at first? That doesn't really sound like him. I thought he would enjoy skydiving!

Megan: I know! I was surprised, too. But Mei did not hesitate to do it.

Jack: Mei was not hesitant? I thought she was extremely cautious.

Megan: Mei really enjoyed it. She wanted to do it again.

Jack: Would you?

Megan: No way! Once was enough for me.

Q. 위 대화문에서 품사의 변화를 보이는 술어는 무엇인가?

① go skydiving ② sound ③ hesitate ④ surprised

정답 : ③

Exercise 1

1. 다음 주어진 문장성분들을 순서대로 배열하시오.

Comp ① ________ ② ________ ③ ________ ④ ________ Mod

Predicate-1 / Subject / Tense / Neg

2. 주어(subject) 또는 명제(proposition)와 같은 하나의 문장성분을 가지고 문장을 형성하는 술어는 어떤 술어인가?

① 1가 술어 ② 2가 술어 ③ 3가 술어 ④ 0가 술어

3. 주어가 명제와 다른 점은?

① 술어 뒤에 위치한다.
② 절로 되어있다.
③ 종속절의 주어가 주절 주어로 이동할 수 있다.
④ 술어 앞에 위치한다.

4. 다음 주어진 문장을 보고 물음에 답하시오.

a. He is intelligent.
b. She is relaxing at home.
c. The door was opened.
d. The mail carrier has just arrived.
e. The medicine does not work.

(1) 위 보기에 주어진 문장 중에서 술어의 품사가 수동형 과거분사인 경우는?

① a ② b ③ c ④ d ⑤ e

(2) 위 보기에 주어진 문장 중에서 술어의 품사가 완료형 과거분사인 경우는?

① a ② b ③ c ④ d ⑤ e

(3) 위 보기에 주어진 문장 중에서 술어의 품사가 형용사인 경우는?

① a ② b ③ c ④ d ⑤ e

(4) 위 보기에 주어진 문장 중에서 술어가 일반동사(동사원형)인 경우는?

① a ② b ③ c ④ d ⑤ e

5. 다음 보기에서 밑 줄친 단어의 문장성분을 찾아 결정하시오.

Ex	Subject	Tense	Neg	Predicate-1	Modifier

(1) Sue exercises regularly.

(2) She does not eat too much.

(3) She does not smoke.

(4) She is not overweight.

(5) She is fit.

(6) She is smiling happily.

6. 다음 주어진 예문을 잘 살펴보고 물음에 답하시오.

a. Judy is outspoken.

b. She is not introverted.

c. Kerry is hard-working.

d. He is not relaxing.

e. The window was broken.

f. It was not repaired yet.

g. Chatty ladies have just arrived.

h. They have not gone yet.

i. Harry and Sally did reconcile.

j. They do not quarrel.

(1) 위 보기에 주어진 문장들은 모두 시제(파란색)와 술어(붉은색)가 분리되어 있다. 하지만 시제와 술어가 하나로 융합될 수 있는 문장이 있다. 이 문장은 어떤 문장인가?

① f ② g ③ h ④ i

(2) 시제와 술어가 하나로 융합될 수 있는 문장이 실제로 융합되면 어떤 문장이 형성되나?

① Harry and Sally reconcile.

② Harry and Sally have reconciled.

③ Harry and Sally reconciled.

④ Harry and Sally had reconciled.

(3) 시제(현재 또는 과거)와 술어가 하나로 융합되기 위해서는 두 가지 조건이 필요하다. 두 가지 조건을 고르시오.

조건1	조건2
a. 술어가 형용사이다.	f. 시제와 술어 사이에 부정어가 있어야 한다.
b. 술어가 현재분사이다.	g. 시제와 술어 사이에 부정어가 없어야 한다.
c. 술어가 수동형 과거분사이다.	
d. 술어가 완료형 과거분사이다.	
e. 술어가 일반동사이다.	

① a, f ② b, g ③ c, g ④ e, g

Coffee Break

False Cognate Words

한국어에서 사용되는 외래어 중에는 영어에서 유래된 단어가 많이 있습니다. 예를 들어 '버스' 또는 '라디오'와 같은 외래어는 영어의 'bus'와 'radio'에서 각각 유래되었습니다. 그런데 영어에서 유래된 외래어 중 일부는 영어 단어와 동일한 의미로 사용되지 않고 다른 의미로 사용되는 경우가 있습니다. 예를 들어 '탈렌트'는 영어단어 'talent'에서 왔지만 재능이라는 의미로 사용되지 않고 '연예인'의 의미로 사용되며, '미팅'은 영어단어 'meeting'에서 왔지만 '회의'의 의미로 사용되기 보다는 '남녀간의 첫 데이트'의 의미로 자주 사용됩니다.

'커닝'도 이러한 예에 속합니다. '커닝'이 영어의 'cunning'에서 왔지만 '교활한'의 의미로 사용되지 않고 '시험에서의 부정행위'의 의미로 사용됩니다. 또 나는 '팝송을 좋아한다'와 같은 문장에서 '팝송'은 영어의 'pop song'에서 유래되었지만 '대중가요'의 의미로 사용되지 않고 '미국노래' 또는 '영국노래'의 의미로 사용됩니다. '매니큐어'도 영어의 'manicure'에서 왔지만 '손을 관리하기'의 의미로 사용되지 않고 '매니큐어액'의 의미로 사용됩니다. '탈렌트', '미팅', '커닝', '팝송', 그리고 '매니큐어'처럼 원래 의미와 다른 의미로 사용되는 외래어를 'false cognate word'라고 합니다.

Quiz. 한국어의 '그랑프리'는 어떤 외국어에서 유래되었을까요?
① 영어 ② 불어 ③ 독어 ④ 스페인어

정답 : ②

Lecture 2 One-Place Predicate with Proposition

Theoretical Explanation

One-Place Predicate with Proposition

Comp	Expletive	Tense	Neg	Predicate-1	Proposition

- Predicate-1(1가 술어) : 주어나 명제와 같은 하나의 문장성분을 가지고 문장을 형성할 수 있는 술어
- Proposition(명제)
  - 술어와 유기적인 의미 관계를 갖는 요소
  - 술어 뒤에 위치한다.
  - 절(clause)로 되어 있다.
  - 종속절(embedded clause)의 주어가 주절(main clause) 주어로 이동할 수 있다.

Sentence Analysis

Example 1 — It is not **likely** that he will arrive on time.

Stage 1

Comp	Expletive	Tense	Neg	Predicate-1
				likely

Stage 2

Comp	Expletive	Tense	Neg	Predicate-1	Comp	Subject	Tense	Neg	Predicate
	It	is	not	likely					

Stage 3

Comp	Expletive	Tense	Neg	Predicate-1	Comp	Subject	Tense	Neg	Predicate	Mod
	It	is	not	likely	that	he	will		arrive	

Stage 4

Comp	Expletive	Tense	Neg	Predicate-1	Comp	Subject	Tense	Neg	Predicate-1	Mod
	It	is	not	likely	that	he	will		arrive	on time

Example 2 — It **seems** that she will arrive on time.

Stage 1

Comp	Expletive	Tense	Neg	Predicate-1
				seems

Stage 2

Comp	Expletive	Tense	Neg	Predicate-1	Comp	Subject	Tense	Neg	Predicate	Mod
	It			seems	that	she	will		arrive	

Stage 3

Comp	Expletive	Tense	Neg	Predicate-1	Comp	Subject	Tense	Neg	Predicate-1	Mod
	It			seems	that	she	will		arrive	on time

Example 3

It is not certain that Bill and Sue will break up.

Stage 1

Comp	Expletive	Tense	Neg	Predicate-1
				certain

Stage 2

Comp	Expletive	Tense	Neg	Predicate-1	Comp	Subject	Tense	Neg	Predicate
	It	is	not	certain					

Stage 3

Comp	Expletive	Tense	Neg	Predicate-1	Comp	Subject	Tense	Neg	Predicate
	It	is	not	certain	that				

Stage 4

Comp	Expletive	Tense	Neg	Predicate-1	Comp	Subject	Tense	Neg	Predicate
	It	is	not	certain	that	Bill and Sue	will		break up

Example 4

It turned out that the newlyweds are divorced.

Stage 1

Comp	Expletive	Tense	Neg	Predicate-1
				turned out

Stage 2

Comp	Expletive	Tense	Neg	Predicate-1	Comp	Subject	Tense	Neg	Predicate-1
	It			turned out					

Stage 3

Comp	Expletive	Tense	Neg	Predicate-1	Comp	Subject	Tense	Neg	Predicate-1
	It			turned out	that				

Stage 4

Comp	Expletive	Tense	Neg	Predicate-1	Comp	Subject	Tense	Neg	Predicate-1
	It			turned out	that	the newlyweds	are		divorced

Example 5

It is likely that they will fall in love.

Stage 1

Comp	Expletive	Tense	Neg	Predicate-1	Comp	Subject	Tense	Neg	Predicate-1
				likely					

Stage 2

Comp	Expletive	Tense	Neg	Predicate-1	Comp	Subject	Tense	Neg	Predicate-1
	It	is		likely					

Stage 3

Comp	Expletive	Tense	Neg	Predicate-1	Comp	Subject	Tense	Neg	Predicate-1
	It	is		likely	that				

Stage 4

Comp	Expletive	Tense	Neg	Predicate-1	Comp	Subject	Tense	Neg	Predicate-1
	It	is		likely	that	they	will		fall in love

Special Tips on Predicates and Tense 2

- Proposition: Proposition is a clause that comes after a one-place predicate. It is similar to a clausal subject in that it is selected by a one-place predicate, but it differs from the clausal subject in that the subject of the embedded clause can move to the subject position of the main clause.

(1) One-place predicate with subject

	It	is	possible	that she will succeed.
1. a.	Expl	Tense	Pred-1	Subj

	*She	is	possible	to succeed.
b.	Subj	Tense	Pred-1	Subj

(2) One-place predicate with proposition

	It	is	likely	that he will succeed.
2. a.	Expl	Tense	Pred-1	Proposition

	He	is	likely	to succeed.
b.	Subj	Tense	Pred-1	Proposition

(3) Examples of one-place predicate with subject

easy, possible, impossible, difficult, hard, probable

(4) Examples of one-place predicate with proposition

seem, prove, turn out, certain, likely, unlikely, happen, appear, sure

Dialogue 2

Bob: What's wrong?

Angie: I need to buy a house soon.

Bob: Isn't that a good thing?

Angie: Well, I was worried that if the real estate market continues on its current trend, the value of the house will fall.

Bob: Oh, I see what you mean.

Angie: Yeah, I'm not sure if this is really the right time to buy a house.

Bob: It's actually a great time to buy a house right now.

Angie: Really?

Bob: Yeah, because it is not likely that the turmoil in the real estate market will persist for a long time.

Angie: I guess the prices are pretty good too.

Bob: Right. The price of this house is at an all time low, but it is expected to go up as the economy improves.

Angie: Oh, really?

Bob: Yes, the turmoil in the real estate market is not likely to persist for a long time.

Angie: How can you be sure?

Bob: I heard from a friend, who is a realtor, that it's likely the market will continue lagging for just another 6 months or so.

Q. 위 대화문에서 종속절의 주어가 주절의 주어로 이동할 수 있도록 허용하는 술어는?

① worried　② likely　③ improve　④ hear

정답 : ②

Exercise 1

Ex

(* = 비문법적인 문장)

1. a. It is impossible that the captive will be released.
   b.*The captive is impossible to be released.
2. a. It is unlikely that the captive will be released.
   b. The captive is unlikely to be released.
3. a. It is possible that he is still alive.
   b.*He is possible to still be alive.
4. a. It is likely that he is still alive.
   b. He is likely to still be alive.
5. a. It is believed that the Korean War has not come to an end.
   b. The Korean War is believed not to have come to an end.

1. 위 예문에 나오는 술어의 공통점은 무엇인가?

① 1가 술어 ② 2가 술어 ③ 3가 술어 ④ 형용사

2. 위 예문에 나오는 술어 중에서 impossible과 possible의 공통점은 무엇인가?

① 주어를 취하는 1가 술어 ② 명제를 취하는 1가 술어

③ 주어와 목적어를 취하는 2가 술어 ④ 주어와 주격보어를 취하는 2가 술어

3. impossible과 possible을 '명제를 취하는 1가 술어'로 간주하지 않고 '주어를 취하는 1가 술어'로 간주한다면 그 근거는 무엇인가?

① 종속절의 주어가 주절 주어로 갈 수 있다.

② 종속절의 주어가 주절 주어로 갈 수 없다.

4. unlikely, likely, believed를 '주어를 취하는 1가 술어'로 간주하지 않고 '명제를 취하는 1가 술어'로 간주한다면 그 근거는 무엇인가?

① 종속절의 주어가 주절 주어로 갈 수 있다.

② 종속절의 주어가 주절 주어로 갈 수 없다.

Exercise 2

Ex	Comp	Expletive	Tense	Neg	Predicate-1	Proposition

1. 다음 문장에서 밑줄 친 단어들의 문장성분을 보기에서 찾아 고르시오.

(1) It is not likely that he will arrive on time.

(2) It seems that she will arrive on time.

(3) It is not certain that Bill and Sue will break up.

(4) It turned out that the newlyweds were divorced.

(5) Is it likely that they have fallen in love?

2. 다음 보기에 있는 두 문장의 상관관계를 잘 살펴보고 이와 같은 패턴이 되도록 주어진 문장을 변형시키시오.

Ex

a. It appears that he is rich. ➡
He appears to be rich.

b. It was likely that the game would end in a tie. ➡
The game was likely to end in a tie.

c. It is certain that he failed the exam. ➡
He is certain to have failed the exam.

(1) a. It appears that the real estate issue has slightly influenced voter sentiment.
b. The real estate issue (   ) (   ) (   ) (   ) influenced voter sentiment.

(2) a. It is not likely that the senator will be defeated in the next election.
b. The senator is not likely (   ) (   ) (   ) in the next election.

(3) a. It turned out that his blood type was A.
b. His blood type turned out (   ) (   ) A.

(4) a. It happened that he saw her yesterday.
b. He happened (   ) (   ) her yesterday.

(5) a. It seems that she was a beauty when young.
b. She seems (   ) (   ) (   ) a beauty when young.

(6) a. It is certain that he passed the exam.
b. He is certain (   ) (   ) (   ) the exam.

Wrap Up

1. One-Place Predicate Sentences

- Comp + Subj + Tense + Neg + Predicate-1
  - Subject(주어) :
    - 술어와 유기적인 의미적 관계를 갖는 요소
    - 술어 앞에 위치함
    - 명사(구) 또는 절로 되어 있음

- Comp + Expletive + Tense + Neg + Predicate-1 + Proposition
  - Proposition(명제) :
    - 술어와 유기적인 의미적 관계를 갖는 요소
    - 술어 뒤에 위치함
    - 절로 되어있음
    - 종속절의 주어가 주절의 주어로 이동할 수 있음

- Structure of One-Place Predicate Sentence with Proposition
  - Comp + Expl + Tense + Pred-1 + Comp + Subj + Tense + Predicate
  - Comp + Subj + Tense + Neg + Pred-1 + _____ + _____ + _____ + Link + Predicate

Memo

UNIT 3

2가 술어에 대한 이해

Two-Place Predicate Sentences

Warm Up

1가 술어(one-place predicate)는 주어(subject)나 명제(proposition)와 같은 하나의 문장성분을 가지고 문장을 형성할 수 있는 술어입니다. 2가 술어(two-place predicate)는 주어 외에 또 하나의 문장성분을 필요로 하는 술어로서 주어를 포함해서 두 개의 문장성분으로 문장을 형성할 수 있는 술어입니다. 3가 술어(three-place predicate)는 문장을 형성하기 위해서 주어를 포함해서 총 세 개의 문장성분을 필요로 하는 술어입니다. 2개의 문장성분을 필요로 하는 2가 술어는 다음과 같이 7가지 유형으로 세분화할 수 있습니다.

Two-Place Predicate Sentences

1. 주어 + (시제) + 2가 술어 + 주격보어
2. 주어 + (시제) + 2가 술어 + 목적어
3. 주어 + (시제) + 2가 술어 + 장소
4. 주어 + (시제) + 2가 술어 + 목적지
5. 주어 + (시제) + 2가 술어 + 출발점
6. 주어 + (시제) + 2가 술어 + 소재
7. 주어 + (시제) + 2가 술어 + 원인

Quiz 1. 2가 술어가 취하는 문장성분

다음 보기에 주어진 예문을 잘 살펴보고 물음에 답하시오.

1. Curtis will become a vocalist.
2. She is studying music.
3. She is happy that her husband supports her.
4. Her studio is located in the suburbs of Seoul.
5. Her studio will move to downtown Seoul.
6. Congratulatory messages will come from her parents.
7. Her new office is full of gifts and flowers.

1. 위 문장에서 파란색 단어의 공통점은 무엇인가?

   ① 1가 술어　　② 2가 술어　　③ 3가 술어　　④ 품사

2. 위 보기에 주어진 문장1~7에서 2가 술어가 주어(subject)와 주격보어(subject complement)를 취하는 문장은?

   ① 1번 문장　　② 2번 문장　　③ 3번 문장　　④ 4번 문장

3. 위 보기에 주어진 문장1~7에서 2가 술어가 주어(subject)와 목적어(object)를 취하는 문장은?

① 1번 문장　② 2번 문장　③ 3번 문장　④ 4번 문장

4. 위 보기에 주어진 문장1~7에서 2가 술어가 주어(subject)와 원인(cause)을 취하는 문장은?

① 1번 문장　② 2번 문장　③ 3번 문장　④ 4번 문장

5. 위 보기에 주어진 문장1~7에서 2가 술어가 주어(subject)와 장소(location)를 취하는 문장은?

① 1번 문장　② 2번 문장　③ 3번 문장　④ 4번 문장

6. 위 보기에 주어진 문장1~7에서 2가 술어가 주어(subject)와 목적지(goal)를 취하는 문장은?

① 4번 문장　② 5번 문장　③ 6번 문장　④ 7번 문장

7. 위 보기에 주어진 문장1~7에서 2가 술어가 주어(subject)와 출처(source)를 취하는 문장은?

① 4번 문장　② 5번 문장　③ 6번 문장　④ 7번 문장

8. 위 보기에 주어진 문장1~7에서 2가 술어가 주어(subject)와 소재(substance)를 취하는 문장은?

① 4번 문장　② 5번 문장　③ 6번 문장　④ 7번 문장

Lecture 1

Basic Sentence Structure

Comp Subject Tense Neg (Link) (Aspect) Predicate

- Comp(보문어) : 문장의 유형을 나타내는 요소, 주절과 종속절을 연결하는 문장 접속사
- Subject(주어) : 술어와 유기적인 의미적 관계를 갖는 요소
- Tense(시제) : 문장의 시제(과거, 현재, 미래)를 나타내는 요소
- Neg(부정어) : 문장을 부정문으로 만드는 요소
- Predicate(술어) : 의미상의 주어를 취하며 문장성분의 수와 종류를 결정하는 요소

Two-Place Predicate Sentences

1. **Comp + Subj + Tense + Neg + Predicate-2 + SC**
2. **Comp + Subj + Tense + Neg + Predicate-2 + Obj**
3. **Comp + Subj + Tense + Neg + Predicate-2 + Loc**
4. Comp + Subj + Tense + Neg + Predicate-2 + Goal
5. Comp + Subj + Tense + Neg + Predicate-2 + Source
6. Comp + Subj + Tense + Neg + Predicate-2 + Substance
7. Comp + Subj + Tense + Neg + Predicate-2 + Cause

- Subject Complement(주격보어) : 주어와 동일한 status를 가지고 있는 요소
- Object(목적어) : 물리적 또는 심리적 행위에 직접적인 대상이 되는 요소
- Location(장소) : 어떤 event가 발생하는 위치

Sentence Analysis

1) Comp + Subject + Tense + Neg + Predicate-2 + Subject Complement

(1)

Joshua	is	a sports major.
Subj	Pred-2	Subject Complement

(2)

He	will	become	a personal trainer.
Subj	Tense	Pred-2	Subject Complement

(3)

His girlfriend	is	called	Susan.
Subj	Tense	Pred-2	Subject Complement

(4)

She	is	becoming	overweight.
Subj	Tense	Pred-2	Subject Complement

(5)

He	is	turning	red.
Subj	Tense	Pred-2	Subject Complement

2) Comp + Subject + Tense + Neg + Predicate-2 + Object

(1)

Joshua	talked to	Susan.
Subj	Pred-2	Obj

(2)

He	does	not	like	her appearance.
Subj	Tense	Neg	Pred-2	Obj

(3)

She	is	reducing	her cholesterol.
Subj	Tense	Pred-2	Obj

(4)

He	is	certain	that her diet will be successful.
Subj	Tense	Pred-2	Obj

(5)

How passionately	he	loves	her!
Comp	Subj	Pred-2	Obj

3) Comp + Subject + Tense + Neg + Predicate-2 + Location

(1) Susan / lives / on the outskirts of New York.
Subj / Pred-2 / Loc

(2) Joshua / resides / in Boston.
Subj / Pred-2 / Loc

(3) Their wedding / will / take place / in downtown New York.
Subj / Tense / Pred-2 / Loc

(4) Their honeymoon house / is / located / in the suburbs of New York.
Subj / Tense / Pred-2 / Loc

(5) How long / will / they / reside / there?
Comp / Tense / Subj / Pred-2 / Loc

Special Tips on Two-Place Predicates

Two-place-predicates basically require two syntactic elements. One of them is a subject and the other is a syntactic element such as a subject complement, object, location, goal, source, substance, or cause.

A subject complement provides information on the subject. The subject complement has the same status as the subject. For example, in the sentence *John is a doctor*, the noun phrase *a doctor* has the same status as the subject *John*, so it is a subject complement.

An object is a syntactic element that is emotionally or physically affected by what the subject performs. For example, in the sentence *Joshua hit Maria* or *Joshua embarrassed Maria*, Maria is physically or emotionally affected by an act that Joshua does, so *Maria* is the object.

A location is where an event takes place. For example, in the sentence *Their wedding was held at Plaza Hotel*, the prepositional phrase *at Plaza Hotel* is the place where the wedding ceremony took place, so the prepositional phrase *at Plaza Hotel* is syntactically a location.

Dialogue 1

Helen: Hey Matt, do you know anyone who goes to the gym regularly? My friend and I are planning to start a gym membership. The gym I would like to go to is located on 17th Avenue.

Matt: Why don't you ask Jeremy? He is a sports major. He works at the gym too.

Helen: Jeremy? Oh, I had no idea. My friend and I need someone who can teach us.

Matt: That's perfect. Jeremy will become a personal trainer. He is in the process of getting his certificate. By the way, who is your friend?

Helen: (It's) my friend Anya. You met her last weekend. Anya really wants to work out. She thinks she's becoming overweight.

Matt: It doesn't ring a bell. What does she look like?

Helen: She came with Jerrod. His girlfriend is called Anya.

Matt: That's too bad that Anya is taken. I thought Jeremy really liked her. He will probably turn red when he hears this.

Q. 위 대화문에서 붉은 색 단어의 공통점은 무엇인가?

① 1가 술어 ② 2가 술어 ③ 3가 술어 ④ 0가 술어

정답 : ②

Exercise 1

1. 문장을 형성하기 위해서 주어(subject) 외에 또 하나의 문장성분을 필요로 하는 술어는?

① 1가 술어　　② 2가 술어　　③ 3가 술어　　④ 품사

2. 다음 보기의 빈칸에 들어갈 수 있는 문장성분을 모두 고르시오.

Ex	Comp	Subject	Tense	Neg	Predicate-2	(　　　　)

① Subject Complement　　② Object　　③ Location　　④ Proposition

3. 2가 술어가 취할 수 있는 문장성분 중에서 주어(subject)와 동일한 status를 가지고 있는 문장성분은?

① Subject Complement　　② Object　　③ Location　　④ Proposition

4. 2가 술어가 취할 수 있는 문장성분 중에서 술어의 어떤 행위(act)나 감정(emotion)의 직접적인 대상이 되는 문장성분은?

① Subject Complement　　② Object　　③ Location　　④ Proposition

5. 2가 술어가 취할 수 있는 문장성분 중에서 어떤 event가 발생하는 장소의 역할을 하는 문장성분은?

① Subject Complement　　② Object　　③ Location　　④ Proposition

Exercise 2

Comp	Subject	Tense	Neg	Predicate-2	Subject Complement

1. 다음 문장에서 단어들의 문장성분을 결정하시오.

(1) His girlfriend is called Susan.

(2) She is becoming overweight.

(3) He is turning red.

Exercise 3

Comp	Subject	Tense	Neg	Predicate-2	Object	Modifier

1. 다음 문장에서 단어들의 문장성분을 결정하시오.

(1) He does not like her appearance.

(2) She is reducing her cholesterol.

(3) How passionately he loves her!

Exercise 4

Comp	Subject	Tense	Neg	Predicate-2	Location	Modifier

1. 다음 문장에서 단어들의 문장성분을 결정하시오.

(1) Their wedding will take place in downtown NewYork.

(2) Their honeymoon house is located in the suburbs of New York.

(3) How long will they reside there?

Exercise 5

1. 다음 문장들은 모두 2가 술어(predicate-2)가 있는 문장들이다. 한 문장을 제외하고 모두 동일한 문장성분으로 되어있다. 문장성분이 나머지 문장과 다른 문장은 어떤 문장인가?

① He feels happy.　　② She remained poor.

③ He grew fat.　　④ She grows vegetables.

2. 다음 문장의 빈칸에 들어갈 적절한 표현을 고르시오.

> The painting was placed (   ).

① yesterday　② on the shelf　③ smoothly　④ for a long time

3. 다음 문장의 빈 칸에 올 수 없는 표현은?

Judy will become (   ).

① a surgeon ② a beauty ③ famous ④ happily

4. 다음 문장의 빈 칸에 올 수 없는 표현은?

Joshua became a famous personal trainer, but his friend remained (   ).

① poorly ② a fisherman ③ poor ④ a farmer

5. 다음 주어진 단어들이 2가 술어(predicate-2)로 사용될 경우 취하는 문장성분이 다른 하나는?

① remain ② feel ③ become ④ live ⑤ turn

6. 다음 문장들이 어떠한 문장성분으로 구성되어있는지 보기에서 고르시오.

Ex

a. Comp + Subj + Tense + Neg + Predicate-2 + SC

b. Comp + Subj + Tense + Neg + Predicate-2 + Obj

c. Comp + Subj + Tense + Neg + Predicate-2 + Loc

① Mizmedi is located in Seoul.

② We were opposed to his plan.

③ He died a millionaire.

Welcome to Our New Home!

Among the many differences that can be found between Korean and American cultures, the way each culture handles greeting new neighbors and hosting or attending housewarming parties is definitely a difference. When a person or family moves into a new home in the States, it is often the surrounding neighbors who initiate contact by dropping by the new person's house to give them food (so they do not have to cook while unpacking their belongings). This is viewed as a great way to strike up a conversation with the new neighbors. In Korea, on the other hand, it is more common for the new person or family to bring rice cakes to their surrounding neighbors as a way to introduce themselves and get to know the people in their neighborhood.

In Korea when people move into a new house, they are expected to give a housewarming party. Newlyweds in particular are expected to do this. It is important that they serve food and drinks and, in return, the people who attend their party bring gifts such as soap, detergent, toilet paper, etc. These are very symbolic gifts in Korean culture. In American culture, however, if newlyweds or new neighbors were to receive these gifts at a housewarming party, they would probably be very puzzled. Such gifts are not nearly as common as flowers, plants, nice bottles of wine, etc.

Quiz. In Korean culture, what is the most common gift that guests bring to a housewarming party?

① tissue ② cake ③ shoes ④ clock

정답 : ①

Lecture 2

1. Comp + Subj + Tense + Neg + Predicate-2 + SC
2. Comp + Subj + Tense + Neg + Predicate-2 + Obj
3. Comp + Subj + Tense + Neg + Predicate-2 + Loc
4. **Comp + Subj + Tense + Neg + Predicate-2 + Goal**
5. **Comp + Subj + Tense + Neg + Predicate-2 + Source**
6. **Comp + Subj + Tense + Neg + Predicate-2 + Substance**
7. **Comp + Subj + Tense + Neg + Predicate-2 + Cause**

Two-Place Predicate Sentences

- Goal(목적지) : 도달하려고 하는 장소
- Source(출발점/출처) : 어떤 여정의 시작점
- Substance(소재) : 어떤 요소를 구성하고 있는 구성성분
- Cause(원인) : 어떤 일의 직접적인 계기가 되는 사건

Sentence Analysis

1) Comp + Subject + Tense + Neg + Predicate-2 + Goal/Source

(1) The newlyweds	will	take a wedding trip	to a foreign country.
Subj	Tense	Pred-2	Goal

(2) They	will	go on a honeymoon	to Europe.
Subj	Tense	Pred-2	Goal

(3) On the first day, | they | will | go | to the Eiffel Tower.
Mod | Subj | Tense | Pred-2 | Goal

(4) On the second day, | they | will | drive | to the British Museum.
Mod | Subj | Tense | Pred-2 | Goal

(5) On the final day, | they | will | come back | from their honeymoon.
Mod | Subj | Tense | Pred-2 | Source

2) Comp + Subject + Tense + Neg + Predicate-2 + Substance

(1) Their new house | is | full of | gifts and flowers from their parents.
Subj | Tense | Pred-2 | Substance

(2) Their living room | is | filled with | suitcases and bags from their honeymoon trip.
Subj | Tense | Pred-2 | Substance

(3) Their refrigerator and kitchen cupboards | are | not | filled with | any food.
Subj | Tense | Neg | Pred-2 | Substance

(4) Their bathroom counter | is | cluttered with | small bottles of shampoo.
Subj | Tense | Pred-2 | Substance

(5) Their bedroom | is | strewn with | their clothing and packages for their friends.
Subj | Tense | Pred-2 | Substance

3) Comp + Subject + Tense + Neg + Predicate-2 + Cause

(1) Joshua and Susan / are / exhausted / from their long flight.
Subj / Tense / Pred-2 / Cause

(2) They / are / relieved / to be home safely.
Subj / Tense / Pred-2 / Cause

(3) They / are / happy / that they are husband and wife.
Subj / Tense / Pred-2 / Cause

(4) They / are / excited / that they are beginning their new life together.
Subj / Tense / Pred-2 / Cause

(5) They / are / happy / that they live in a good neighborhood.
Subj / Tense / Pred-2 / Cause

Special Tips on Two-Place Predicates

A goal is a place that one is trying to reach. It differs from a location in that it is not a place where something is currently happening, but rather a place that we want to get to by travelling a certain distance. For example, in the sentence 'He is going to Paris,' 'Paris' is not a place where something is taking place. It is the place that the subject is trying to reach, so it is a goal.

A source is a place from which one is coming. For example, in the sentence 'The newlyweds have just arrived from their honeymoon trip in Paris,' Paris is not the place they are going to but the place they are coming from, so it is a source.

A substance is a material that something is composed of or filled with. For example, in the sentence 'The pillow is stuffed with feathers,' feathers are the kind of material that the pillow is filled with. So the word 'feathers' indicates a substance.

A cause is something that brings about a certain consequence. For example, in the sentence 'He was blamed for the mistake,' his mistake is what caused him to be blamed, so it is a cause.

Dialogue 2

Sue: John and Mary's wedding was wonderful!

Bob: Yeah, and did you see all those presents?

Sue: I'm not surprised. Their new house is full of gifts and flowers from their parents.

Bob: Wow! John and Mary make a great couple. They are happy that they are husband and wife. You know they waited quite a while to get married.

Sue: Really? I didn't know that. Well, in that case, I hope they're going somewhere special for their honeymoon.

Bob: Actually they are. The newlyweds will take a wedding trip to another country. I think they said Italy. They're planning to take a 2 week tour all over they country, and every day they'll be staying in a different city.

Sue: Really? That sounds amazing, but very fast paced.

Bob: You know John and Mary. They like to be on the go. They leave this Saturday and will be gone for 14 days, but that includes travel to and from there. On the final day, they will come back from their honeymoon.

Sue: Oh, so their actual vacation time will be shorter than 2 weeks.

Bob: Yes. With travel time and the time difference, it's actually more like 9 or 10 days.

Q. 위 대화문에서 원인(cause)을 취하는 2가 술어는 무엇인가?

① full ② happy ③ take a wedding trip ④ come back

정답 : ②

Exercise 1

1. 다음 보기의 빈칸에 들어갈 수 있는 문장성분을 모두 고르시오.

> **Ex** Comp Subject Tense Neg Predicate-2 ( )

① Goal ② Source ③ Substance ④ Cause ⑤ Expletive

2. 2가 술어(predicate-2)가 취할 수 있는 문장성분 중에서 주어가 도달하려고 하는 장소의 역할을 하는 문장성분은?

① Goal ② Source ③ Substance ④ Cause ⑤ Expletive

3. 2가 술어(predicate-2)가 취할 수 있는 문장성분 중에서 어떤 여정의 시작점이 되는 문장성분은?

① Goal ② Source ③ Substance ④ Cause ⑤ Expletive

4. 2가 술어(predicate-2)가 취할 수 있는 문장성분 중에서 어떤 사물을 구성하는 요소의 역할을 하는 문장성분은?

① Goal ② Source ③ Substance ④ Cause ⑤ Expletive

5. 2가 술어(predicate-2)가 취할 수 있는 문장성분 중에서 어떤 사건(event), 행위(act), 또는 감정(emotion)의 원인이 되는 문장성분은?

① Goal ② Source ③ Substance ④ Cause ⑤ Expletive

Exercise 2

1. 다음 문장에서 단어들의 문장성분을 결정하시오.

Comp	Subject	Tense	Neg	Predicate-2	Goal / Source

① They will go to the Eiffel Tower.

② They will drive to the British Museum.

③ When will they come back from their honeymoon?

Exercise 3

1. 다음 문장에서 밑줄친 단어들의 문장성분을 결정하시오.

Comp	Subject	Tense	Neg	Predicate-2	Substance	Modifier

① Their refrigerator and kitchen cupboards are not filled with any food.

② Their bathroom counter is cluttered with small bottles of shampoo and soaps.

③ Their bedroom is strewn with their clothing and packages for their friends.

Exercise 4

1. 다음 문장에서 단어들의 문장성분을 결정하시오.

Comp	Subject	Tense	Neg	Predicate-2	Cause

① Joshua and Susan are exhausted from their long flight.

Exercise 5

1. 다음 보기에 주어진 두 문장의 밑줄 친 부분의 문장성분은 무엇인가?

Ex
a. I was sorry that he failed the exam.
b. I was sure that he would fail the exam.

① a: 원인, b: 원인　　② a: 목적어, b: 목적어

③ a: 원인, b: 목적어　　④ a: 목적어, b: 원인

2. 다음 문장들이 어떠한 문장성분으로 구성되어있는지 보기에서 고르시오.

① Comp + Subj + Tense + Neg + Predicate-2 + Goal

② Comp + Subj + Tense + Neg + Predicate-2 + Source

③ Comp + Subj + Tense + Neg + Predicate-2 + Substance

④ Comp + Subj + Tense + Neg + Predicate-2 + Cause

(1) New York is far from Chicago.

(2) The bus was crowded with passengers.

(3) Sue is worried that her son may fail the exam.

(4) She was surprised at the result.

(5) The poor man left for his hometown.

(6) The glass is full of water.

(7) The musician flew from Hawaii.

Wrap Up

Basic Sentence Structure

Comp Subject Tense Neg (Link) (Aspect) Predicate

- Comp(보문어) : 문장의 유형을 결정하는 요소, 주절과 종속절을 연결하는 문장접속사
- Subject(주어) : 술어와 유기적인 의미적 관계를 갖는 요소
- Tense(시제) : 문장의 시제(현재, 미래, 과거)를 나타내는 요소
- Neg(부정어) : 문장을 부정문으로 만드는 요소
- Predicate(술어) : 의미상의 주어를 취하며 문장성분의 수와 종류를 결정하는 요소

Two-Place Predicate Sentences

1. Comp + Subj + Tense + Neg + Predicate-2 + SC
2. Comp + Subj + Tense + Neg + Predicate-2 + Obj
3. Comp + Subj + Tense + Neg + Predicate-2 + Loc
4. Comp + Subj + Tense + Neg + Predicate-2 + Goal
5. Comp + Subj + Tense + Neg + Predicate-2 + Source
6. Comp + Subj + Tense + Neg + Predicate-2 + Substance
7. Comp + Subj + Tense + Neg + Predicate-2 + Cause

Memo

UNIT 4

3가 술어에 대한 이해

Three-Place Predicate Sentences

Warm Up

1가 술어(one-place predicate)는 주어(subject)나 명제(proposition)와 같은 하나의 문장성분을 가지고 문장을 형성할 수 있는 술어입니다. 2가 술어(two-place predicate)는 문장을 형성하기 위해서 주어 외에 또 하나의 문장성분을 필요로 하는 술어로서 총 두 개의 문장성분을 필요로 하는 술어입니다. 3가 술어(three-place predicate)는 주어 외에 두 개의 문장성분을 더 필요로 하는 술어로서 총 세 개의 문장성분을 필요로 하는 술어입니다. 3가 술어는 다음과 같이 7가지 유형으로 세분화 할 수 있습니다.

Three-Place Predicate Sentences

1. 주어 + (시제) + 3가 술어 + 직접목적어 + 간접목적어
2. 주어 + (시제) + 3가 술어 + 간접목적어 + 직접목적어
3. 주어 + (시제) + 3가 술어 + 목적어 + 출발점/출처
4. 주어 + (시제) + 3가 술어 + 목적어 + 장소
5. 주어 + (시제) + 3가 술어 + 목적어 + 원인
6. 주어 + (시제) + 3가 술어 + 목적어 + 소재
7. 주어 + (시제) + 3가 술어 + 목적어 + 목적격보어

Quiz 1 3가 술어가 취하는 문장성분

다음 보기에 주어진 예문을 잘 살펴보고 물음에 답하시오.

Ex

1. The university will confer an honorary doctorate upon Mr. Kim.
2. He will supply the school with new desks and chairs.
3. The students will also receive financial aid from him.
4. The university will place a commemorative statue of him in front of the library.
5. The students thank him for his generosity.
6. They covered his car with ribbons and flowers.
7. They think of him as a mentor.

1. 위 문장에서 파란색 단어의 공통점은 무엇인가?

① 1가 술어 ② 2가 술어 ③ 3가 술어 ④ 품사

2. 위 보기에 주어진 문장 중에서 3가 술어가 직접목적어와 간접목적어를 취하는 문장은?

① 1번 문장 ② 2번 문장 ③ 3번 문장 ④ 4번 문장

3. 위 보기에 주어진 문장에서 3가 술어가 간접목적어와 직접목적어를 취하는 문장은?

① 1번 문장 ② 2번 문장 ③ 3번 문장 ④ 4번 문장

4. 위 보기에 주어진 문장에서 3가 술어가 목적어와 출처(source)를 취하는 문장은?

① 1번 문장 ② 2번 문장 ③ 3번 문장 ④ 4번 문장

5. 위 보기에 주어진 문장에서 3가 술어가 목적어와 장소(location)를 취하는 문장은?

① 1번 문장 ② 2번 문장 ③ 3번 문장 ④ 4번 문장

6. 위 보기에 주어진 문장에서 3가 술어가 목적어와 원인(cause)을 취하는 문장은?

① 4번 문장 ② 5번 문장 ③ 6번 문장 ④ 7번 문장

7. 위 보기에 주어진 문장에서 3가 술어가 목적어와 소재(substance)를 취하는 문장은?

① 4번 문장 ② 5번 문장 ③ 6번 문장 ④ 7번 문장

8. 위 보기에 주어진 문장에서 3가 술어가 목적어와 목적격보어를 취하는 문장은?

① 4번 문장 ② 5번 문장 ③ 6번 문장 ④ 7번 문장

Lecture 1

Basic Sentence Structure

Comp Subject Tense Neg (Link) (Aspect) Predicate

- Comp(보문어) : 문장의 유형을 나타내는 요소, 주절과 종속절을 연결하는 문장접속사
- Subject(주어) : 술어와 유기적인 의미적 관계를 갖는 요소
- Tense(시제) : 문장의 시제(과거, 현재, 미래)를 나타내는 요소
- Neg(부정어) : 문장을 부정문으로 만드는 요소
- Predicate(술어) : 의미상의 주어를 취하는 요소, 문장성분의 수와 종류를 결정하는 요소

Three-Place Predicate Sentences

1. **Comp + Subj + Tense + Neg + Predicate-3 + DO + IO**
2. **Comp + Subj + Tense + Neg + Predicate-3 + IO + DO**
3. **Comp + Subj + Tense + Neg + Predicate-3 + Obj + Source**
4. **Comp + Subj + Tense + Neg + Predicate-3 + Obj + Loc**
5. Comp + Subj + Tense + Neg + Predicate-3 + Obj + Cause
6. Comp + Subj + Tense + Neg + Predicate-3 + Obj + Substance
7. Comp + Subj + Tense + Neg + Predicate-3 + Obj + Object Complement

- Direct Object(직접목적어) : 물리적 또는 심리적 행위에 직접적인 대상이 되는 요소
- Indirect Object(간접목적어) : 물리적 또는 심리적 행위에 간접적인 대상이 되는 요소
- Source(출처/출발점) : 어떤 여정이나 이동의 출발점이 되는 요소
- Location(장소) : 어떤 event가 발생하는 위치
- Cause(원인) : 어떤 일의 직접적인 계기가 되는 사건
- Substance(소재) : 어떤 요소를 구성하고 있는 구성성분
- Object Complement(목적격 보어) : 목적어와 동일한 status를 지니고 있는 요소

Sentence Analysis

1) Comp + Subj + Tense + Neg + Predicate-3 + DO + IO

(1)

A university	will	confer	a medal	upon a retiring professor.
Subj	Tense	Pred-3	DO	IO

(2)

He	will	deliver	a farewell speech	to his colleagues and students.
Subj	Tense	Pred-3	DO	IO

(3)

The students	seek	advice and tips	of the speaker.
Subj	Pred-3	DO	IO

(4)

The professor	offers	his thanks	to the guests gathered at the ceremony.
Subj	Pred-3	DO	IO

2) Comp + Subj + Tense + Neg + Predicate-3 + IO + DO

(1)

The professor	had	reminded	the students	to study hard.
Subj	Tense	Pred-3	IO	DO

(2)

He	will	offer	the students	advice and tips on how to live a meaningful life.
Subj	Tense	Pred-3	IO	DO

(3)

He	promised	the students	to continue to help them with their studies.
Subj	Pred-3	IO	DO

(4)

He	encourages	them	to major in promising areas.
Subj	Pred-3	IO	DO

3) Comp + Subj + Tense + Neg + Predicate-3 + Obj + Source

(1) The students	have	received	books	from the benefactor.
Subj	Tense	Pred-3	Obj	Source

(2) They	will	also	get	a laptop computer	from him.
Subj	Tense	Mod	Pred-3	Obj	Source

(3) One of them	will	obtain	a scholarship	from the sponsor.
Subj	Tense	Pred-3	Obj	Source

(4) The students	have	received	a lot of assistance	from him.
Subj	Tense	Pred-3	Obj	Source

4) Comp + Subj + Tense + Neg + Predicate-3 + Obj + Location

(1) One male student	had	put	a laptop computer	on the table.
Subj	Tense	Pred-3	Object	Location

(2) Another male student	relocated	the laptop computer	to the shelf.
Subj	Pred-3	Object	Location

(3) A female student	locked	the laptop computer	in her desk.
Subj	Pred-3	Object	Location

(4) She	will	attach	a webcam	to the laptop computer.
Subj	Tense	Pred-3	Object	Location

Special Tips on Three-Place Predicates

A three-place predicate requires three syntactic elements to form a sentence. It requires a subject and two more sentence elements. The two additional elements are a direct object and an indirect object, an indirect object and a direct object, an object and a source, an object and a location, an object and a cause, an object and a substance, and an object and an object complement.

A source is something from which something else comes, or from which something is gotten. For example, in the sentence *I got a gift from Judy,* Judy is the person that I got a gift from, so *from Judy* indicates a source.

Dialogue 1

Jake: Did you hear? Your university will receive a huge amount of money from a very generous donor.

Sally: What? How come I'm the last one hearing about this? Who is the donor?

Jake: John James Suillivan III. He just won the Nobel Peace Prize, and he has donated 100 million dollars to his university. In fact, at the graduation ceremony next week, he will deliver a speech to those gathered at the ceremony.

Sally: That's great news! My university will have a bigger budget for everything.

Jake: Yes, I also heard that the rich man will supply the students with English books, too. And as a small token of gratitude your university will donate 5,000 notebook computers to local kindergartens nearby.

Sally: Where do they locate so many computers?

Jake: From a small company going out of business.

Sally: What a great deal!

Q. 위 대화문에서 나오는 술어 중에서 간접목적어와 직접목적어를 취하는 술어는?

① donate ② deliver ③ supply ④ locate

정답 : ③

Exercise 1

1. 다음 문장에서 술어가 몇 가 술어인지 고르시오.

(1) She cannot keep him from laughing. (그녀는 그에게 웃음을 막을 수 없다.)

① 1가 술어 ② 2가 술어 ③ 3가 술어 ④ 0가 술어

(2) He can hardly keep from smoking. (그는 흡연을 금할 수 없다.)

① 1가 술어 ② 2가 술어 ③ 3가 술어 ④ 0가 술어

(3) Jina promised him that she would arrive before noon. (지나는 그에게 정오 전에 도착하겠다고 약속했다.)

① 1가 술어 ② 2가 술어 ③ 3가 술어 ④ 0가 술어

(4) Jina promised that she would arrive before noon. (지나는 정오 전에 도착하겠다고 약속했다.)

① 1가 술어 ② 2가 술어 ③ 3가 술어 ④ 0가 술어

2. 다음 보기에 주어진 술어들이 공통으로 형성할 수 있는 문장의 유형은?

Ex remind, rob, prevent, keep from, inform, warn, advise, rid

① Comp + Subj + Tense + Neg + Predicate−3 + DO + IO
② Comp + Subj + Tense + Neg + Predicate−3 + IO + DO
③ Comp + Subj + Tense + Neg + Predicate−3 + Obj + Source
④ Comp + Subj + Tense + Neg + Predicate−3 + Obj + Loc

3. 다음 보기에 주어진 술어들이 타동사(transitive verb)로 사용될 경우 형성할 수 있는 문장의 유형은?

> **Ex** put, place, locate, hide, set, seat, situate, position

① Comp + Subj + Tense + Neg + Predicate−3 + DO + IO

② Comp + Subj + Tense + Neg + Predicate−3 + IO + DO

③ Comp + Subj + Tense + Neg + Predicate−3 + Obj + Source

④ Comp + Subj + Tense + Neg + Predicate−3 + Obj + Loc

4. 다음 문장들이 보기에 어떤 유형에 해당하는지 고르시오?

> **Ex**
> a. Comp + Subj + Tense + Neg + Predicate-3 + DO + IO
> b. Comp + Subj + Tense + Neg + Predicate-3 + IO + DO
> c. Comp + Subj + Tense + Neg + Predicate-3 + Obj + Source
> d. Comp + Subj + Tense + Neg + Predicate-3 + Obj + Loc

(1) Cindy received a big sum of retirement allowance from her company.

① a　　② b　　③ c　　④ d

(2) She will deposit her retirement allowance in the First Bank.

① a　　② b　　③ c　　④ d

(3) The President of a foreign country delivered a speech to the students of a university of Korea.

① a ② b ③ c ④ d

(4) He offered the students advice and tips on how to live a meaningful life.

① a ② b ③ c ④ d

Coffee Break

Sleep Expressions in American culture

In American culture, there are a number of common idiomatic expressions to talk about sleep. These usually refer to the time, depth, or behavior displayed during one's sleep.

If a person is said to sleep like a cat, or "cat nap," this means the individual takes short naps instead of a long restful sleep. He probably wakes up during the night many more times than an average person.

"Sleeping like a dog" means that the slightest movement or sound automatically wakes the individual up. He becomes as watchful as a watch-dog in his sleep. This individual always complains of being tired from not getting enough sleep.

'Sleep walkers' are individuals who unconsciously wake up at night without being aware of it and go places, prepare food, eat it and go back to sleep without remembering anything about it the next morning. A woman even murdered her husband and went free in court because it was believed that she was sleep walking when she committed the offence, so it was not considered to be a crime.

Finally, people who "sleep like a bear" are people who sleep very well. Bears are hibernators, which means that they sleep through the winter months. For this reason, people who have long uninterrupted sleep are said to "sleep like a bear."

Quiz. What kind of sleeper are you?

① cat napper ② sleep like a dog ③ sleep walker ④ sleep like a bear

정답 : ?

Lecture 2

Three-Place Predicate Sentences

1. Comp + Subj + Tense + Neg + Predicate-3 + DO + IO
2. Comp + Subj + Tense + Neg + Predicate-3 + IO + DO
3. Comp + Subj + Tense + Neg + Predicate-3 + Obj + Source
4. Comp + Subj + Tense + Neg + Predicate-3 + Obj + Loc
5. **Comp + Subj + Tense + Neg + Predicate-3 + Obj + Cause**
6. **Comp + Subj + Tense + Neg + Predicate-3 + Obj + Substance**
7. **Comp + Subj + Tense + Neg + Predicate-3 + Obj + Object Complement**

- Cause(원인) : 어떤 일의 직접적인 계기가 되는 사건
- Substance(소재) : 어떤 요소를 구성하고 있는 구성성분
- Object Complement(목적격 보어) : 목적어와 동일한 status를 지니고 있는 요소

Sentence Analysis

1) Comp + Subj + Tense + Neg + Predicate-3 + Obj + Cause

(1)

A teacher	had	scolded	some students	for being late to class.
Subj	Tense	Pred-3	Object	Cause

(2)

He	praised	other students	for studying hard.
Subj	Pred-3	Object	Cause

(3) Parents	will	rebuke	the lazy students	for poor grades.
Subj	Tense	Pred-3	Object	Cause

(4) They	will	reward	the hard-working students	for good grades.
Subj	Tense	Pred-3	Object	Cause

2) Comp + Subj + Tense + Neg + Predicate-3 + Obj + Substance

(1) A maid working in a hotel	has	replaced	an old blanket	with a new one.
Subj	Tense	Pred-3	Object	Substance

(2) She	had	stuffed	the new blanket	with cotton.
Subj	Tense	Pred-3	Object	Substance

(3) The hotel manager	has	replaced	the solid soap in the bathroom	with liquid soap.
Subj	Tense	Pred-3	Object	Substance

(4) Guests	substituted	powdered soap	for liquid soap.
Subj	Pred-3	Object	Substance

3) Comp + Subj + Tense + Neg + Predicate-3 + Obj + Obiect Complement

(1) The sailors	will	name	the ship	the Titanic.
Subj	Tense	Pred-3	Object	Object Complement

(2) They	may	elect	Geoff	as captain.
Subj	Tense	Pred-3	Object	Object Complement

(3) The Captain	has	appointed	Tony	First Mate.
Subj	Tense	Pred-3	Object	Object Complement

(4) Tony	thought of	his appointment	as an honor.
Subj	Pred-3	Object	Object Complement

(5) He	made	other sailors	comfortable and safe.
Subj	Pred-3	Object	Object Complement

Special Tips on Three-Place Predicates

A three-place-predicate requires three syntactic elements to form a sentence. It requires a subject and two more elements. The two additional elements are a direct object and an indirect object, an indirect object and a direct object, an object and a source, an object and a location, an object and a cause, an object and a substance, and an object and an object complement.

A substance is some kind of material of which something is composed. For example, in the sentence *He filled his bags with books*, books are the things with which the bags are filled, so the word 'with books' indicates a substance.

3. 다음 보기에 주어진 술어들이 타동사로 사용될 경우 형성할 수 있는 문장의 유형은?

have(사역동사), make(사역동사), let(사역동사), name,
nominate, appoint, think of, regard, call, hear

① Comp + Subj + Tense + Neg + Predicate−3 + Obj + Cause

② Comp + Subj + Tense + Neg + Predicate−3 + Obj + Substance

③ Comp + Subj + Tense + Neg + Predicate−3 + Obj + Obiect Complement

④ Comp + Subj + Tense + Neg + Predicate−2 + Substance

4. 다음 보기에 주어진 술어들이 타동사로 사용될 경우 형성할 수 있는 문장의 유형은?

fill, plenish, charge(장전하다), replace, stuff, substitute, load, pack

① Comp + Subj + Tense + Neg + Predicate−3 + Obj + Cause

② Comp + Subj + Tense + Neg + Predicate−3 + Obj + Substance

③ Comp + Subj + Tense + Neg + Predicate−3 + Obj + Obiect Complement

④ Comp + Subj + Tense + Neg + Predicate−2 + Substance

5. 다음 문장들이 보기에 어떤 유형에 해당하는지 고르시오?

a. Comp + Subj + Tense + Neg + Predicate-3 + Obj + Cause
b. Comp + Subj + Tense + Neg + Predicate-3 + Obj + Substance
c. Comp + Subj + Tense + Neg + Predicate-3 + Obj + Obiect Complement
d. Comp + Subj + Tense + Neg + Predicate-2 + Substance

(1) The citizens will censure the Government for maladministration.

① a ② b ③ c ④ d

(2) Betty had stuffed a pillow with feathers.

① a ② b ③ c ④ d

(3) The doctor called me a heavy smoker.

① a ② b ③ c ④ d

(4) Mr. Brown gave him a long lecture for being lazy.

① a ② b ③ c ④ d

(5) John had his car repaired.

① a ② b ③ c ④ d

(6) We can substitute oil for coal.

① a ② b ③ c ④ d

6. 다음 보기에 주어진 문장들은 make 동사와 have 동사가 주어, 목적어, 그리고 목적격보어를 취하는 3가 술어로 사용되는 예들이다. 주어진 예문을 잘 살펴보고 물음에 답하시오. (* = 비문법적인 문장)

① John can make himself understood in English.
② Mary had her car repaired.
③ *His joke made the children laughing heartily.
④ The comedian had her laughing heartily.
⑤ The boss made his secretary finish the work.
⑥ The professor had his students do their best.

(1) 3가 술어로 사용되는 make 동사가 목적격보어로 취할 수 있는 동사의 형태를 있는 대로 고르시오.

① 수동형과거분사 ② 현재분사 ③ 동사원형 ④ 완료형 과거분사

(2) 3가 술어로 사용되는 have 동사가 목적격보어로 취할 수 있는 동사의 형태를 있는 대로 고르시오.

① 수동형과거분사 ② 현재분사 ③ 동사원형 ④ 완료형 과거분사

Wrap Up

Three-Place Predicate Sentences

1. Comp + Subj + Tense + Neg + Predicate-3 + DO + IO
2. Comp + Subj + Tense + Neg + Predicate-3 + IO + DO
3. Comp + Subj + Tense + Neg + Predicate-3 + Obj + Source
4. Comp + Subj + Tense + Neg + Predicate-3 + Obj + Loc
5. Comp + Subj + Tense + Neg + Predicate-3 + Obj + Cause
6. Comp + Subj + Tense + Neg + Predicate-3 + Obj + Substance
7. Comp + Subj + Tense + Neg + Predicate-3 + Obj + Obiect Complement

- Direct Object(직접목적어) : 물리적 또는 심리적 행위에 직접적인 대상이 되는 요소
- Indirect Object(간접목적어) : 물리적 또는 심리적 행위에 간접적인 대상이 되는 요소
- Source(출처/출발점) : 어떤 여정이나 이동의 출발점이 되는 요소
- Location(장소) : 어떤 event가 발생하는 위치
- Cause(원인) : 어떤 일의 직접적인 계기가 되는 사건
- Substance(소재) : 어떤 요소를 구성하고 있는 구성성분
- Object Complement(목적격 보어) : 목적어와 동일한 status를 지니고 있는 요소

UNIT 5

품사의 호환성

Changeability of Parts of Speech

Warm Up

술어(predicate)는 문장을 형성하는 데 가장 핵심이 되는 요소로서 기본적으로 의미상의 주어를 취하는 요소이다. 술어의 품사는 일반동사, 진행형 현재분사, 수동형 과거분사, 완료형 과거분사, 형용사, 전치사 등 다양한 품사가 가능하다.

술어의 품사(parts of speech of predicates)

(1) 일반동사(lexical verb)

(2) 진행형 현재분사(progressive participle)

(3) 수동형 과거분사(passive participle)

(4) 완료형 과거분사(perfect participle)

(5) 형용사(adjective)

(6) 전치사(preposition)

술어의 품사는 이처럼 다양하며 술어가 일반동사일 때는 시제를 나타낼 수 있다. 술어의 품사는 유동성이 있으며 따라서 술어는 동사에서 형용사로 변화될 수 있고 동사에서 명사로 변화될 수도 있다.

Quiz 1. 품사의 호환성

다음 보기에 주어진 예문을 잘 살펴보고 물음에 답하시오.

Ex

1. a. He did not succeed.
   b. He was not successful.
2. a. The Egyptians respected black cats.
   b. The Egyptians were respectful of black cats.
3. a. Children depend on their parents.
   b. Children are dependent on parents
4. a. She suspected her husband.
   b. She was suspicious of her husband.

1. 위 보기에서 a번 문장의 b번 문장으로의 변화는 어떤 변화인가?

① 술어의 품사의 변화　　② 시제의 변화

③ 술어의 결합가(valency)의 변화　　④ 상(aspect)의 변화

결합가: 술어가 필요로 하는 문장성분의 수

2. 술어가 동사에서 형용사로 바뀌게 되면 'were', 'was' 또는 'are'와 같은 be-동사가 추가되는 이유는 무엇인가?

① 문장의 의미를 바꾸기 위해서

② 형용사 술어가 나타낼 수 없는 시제를 나타내기 위해서

③ 형용사 술어가 나타낼 수 없는 상(aspect)을 나타내기 위해서

④ 문장의 유형을 바꾸기 위해서

Lecture 1

Basic Sentence Structure

Definition of 7 Basic Sentence Elements

Comp	Subject	Tense	Neg	(Link)	(Aspect)	Predicate

- Comp(보문어) : 문장의 유형을 나타내는 요소, 주절과 종속절을 연결하는 문장접속사
- Subject(주어) : 술어와 유기적인 의미적 관계를 갖는 요소
- Tense(시제) : 문장의 시제(과거, 현재, 미래)를 나타내는 요소
- Neg(부정어) : 문장을 부정문으로 만드는 요소
- Link(연결어) : 두 문장성분의 연결을 가능하게 하는 요소
- Aspect(상) : 진행이나 완료를 나타내는 요소
- Predicate(술어) : 의미상의 주어를 취하는 요소, 문장성분의 수와 종류를 결정하는 요소

Changeability of Parts of Speech of Predicates

- 1가 술어: Subject + (Tense) + Pred-1(Verb) → Subject + Tense + Pred-1(Adjective)

(1)

The Prime minister	did	not	succeed	on his first trial of the speech.
Subj	Tense	Neg	Pred-1	Mod

(2)

He	was	not	successful	on his second trail of the speech,	either.
Subj	Tense	Neg	Pred-1	Mod1	Mod2

(3)

He	did	not	hesitate	at all.
Subj	Tense	Neg	Pred-1	Mod

(4) He	was	not	hesitant	over the choice between the two humors.
Subj	Tense	Neg	Pred-1	Mod

(5) He	succeeded	on his third trial of the speech.
Subj	Pred-1	Mod

(6) His bodyguards	did	not	relax	until the end of the event.
Subj	Tense	Neg	Pred-1	Mod

(7) They	were	not	relaxed	even after the end of the event.
Subj	Tense	Neg	Pred-1	Mod

- **2가 술어: Subject + (Tense) + Pred-2(Verb) + Obj**

  ➡ Subject + Tense + Pred-2(Adjective/of) + Obj

(1) The audience	respected	the speaker.
Subj	Pred-2	Obj

(2) They	were	even	respectful of	his attendants.
Subj	Tense	Mod	Pred-2	Obj

(3) His opinions	represented	those of underprivileged people.
Subj	Pred-2	Obj

(4) His opinions	are	also	representative of
Subj	Tense	Mod	Pred-2

the opinions of the middle-income bracket.
Obj

(5) The rhetorical style of his speech	typified	the famous political leaders.
Subj	Pred-2	Obj

(6) Dynamic use of gestures	is	typical of	his speech.
Subj	Tense	Pred-2	Obj

(7) Many people	support	him.
Subj	Pred-2	Obj

(8) Minors	are	more strongly	supportive of	him.
Subj	Tense	Mod	Pred-2	Obj

- **2가 술어: Subject + (Tense) + Pred-2(Verb) + Obj**

  ➡ Subject + Tense + Pred-2(Adjective/to) + Obj

(1) His humor	interested	most of the audience.
Subj	Pred-2	Obj

(2) His jokes	were	particularly	interesting	to the female listeners.
Subj	Tense	Mod	Pred-2	Obj

(3) The strong spot-lights of the auditorium	disturbed	the speaker.
Subj	Pred-2	Obj

(4) The noisy children	were	even more	disturbing	to him.
Subj	Tense	Mod	Pred-2	Obj

(5) A suspect person	suddenly	frightened	the politician.
Subj	Mod	Pred-2	Obj

(6) His bizarre gesture | was | even | frightening | to his bodyguards.
Subj | Tense | Mod | Pred-2 | Obj

(7) We | worried | that he would harm the speaker.
Subj | Pred-2 | Cause

(8) The bodyguards | were | even more | worried | that he would be wounded.
Subj | Tense | Mod | Pred-2 | Cause

Special Tips on the Changeability of Parts of Speech of Predicates

- Parts of Speech of Predicates

(1) Lexical verbs

Ex

She	does	not	smoke.
Subj	Tense	Neg	Pred-1

(2) Progressive participles

Ex

She	is	smiling.
Subj	Tense	Pred-1

(3) Passive participles

Ex

The packet	was	delivered	yesterday.
Subj	Tense	Pred-1	Mod

(4) Perfect participles

Ex

The delegation	has	arrived.
Subj	Tense	Pred-1

(5) Adjectives

Ex

She	is	gorgeous.
Subj	Tense	Pred-1

(6) Preposition

Ex

I	am	against	John breaking up with his girlfriend.
Subj	Tense	Pred-2	Obj

Changeability of Parts of Speech of Predicates

When verb predicates are changed to adjectives, compensatory tense indicators such as *am, are, is, was, or were* are used to represent tense since adjectives do not indicate tense.

Examples of Compensatory Tense Indicators

Ex

1\. a. The suspect hesitated at first.

The suspect	hesitated	at first.
Subj	Pred-1	Mod

b. The suspect was hesitant at first.

The suspect	was	hesitant	at first.
Subj	Tense	Pred-1	Mod

2\. a. John worries that he may fail the exam.

John	worries	that he may fail the exam.
Subj	Pred-1	Cause

b. John is worried that he may fail the exam.

John	is	worried	that he may fail the exam.
Subj	Tense	Pred-1	Cause

3\. a. The heavy smoker resolved to stop smoking.

The heavy smoker	resolved	to stop smoking.
Subj	Pred-1	Obj

b. The heavy smoker was resolved to stop smoking.

The heavy smoker	was	resolved	to stop smoking.
Subj	Tense	Pred-1	Obj

Dialogue 1

Bob: Do you plan to vote in the student elections?

Sue: Yeah, definitely. We need a leader who can really change things for the better.

Bob: Have you thought about who you're going to vote for?

Sue: I was thinking about Tom. His opinions represent those of other students.

Bob: I agree. His opinions are representative of those of other students. But will he be able to persuade the administration?

Sue: I think so.

Bob: How was his speech that he delivered yesterday?

Sue: It was great, especially the part about promoting more volunteer activities.

Bob: Oh? What did he say?

Sue: Well, he mentioned different approaches, but he said one way works best for him. His idea interested me.

Bob: His idea was interesting to you? Wow!

Sue: That's why I stayed a little longer.

Bob: I wish him good luck.

Sue: Me, too.

Q. 위 대화문에서 품사의 호환을 보이는 단어는 무엇인가? (둘을 고르시오)

① need ② represent ③ deliver ④ interest

정답: ②, ④

Exercise 1

1. 보기 A에 주어진 두 문장의 상관관계를 잘 살펴보고 이와 비슷한 패턴이 되도록 적절한 단어를 보기 B에서 골라 빈 칸을 채우시오.

Ex A

a. He finally died at the age of 68. ➡

b. He was finally dead at the age of 68.

Ex B

hesitant, successful, behaved, married, dead

(1) Charles did not succeed in bringing rain. ➡ Charles was not (   ) in bringing rain.

(2) The child hesitated at first. ➡ The child was (   ) at first.

(3) Judy married right after graduation. ➡ Judy was (   ) right after graduation.

(4) The veteran soldier finally died. ➡ The veteran soldier was finally (   ).

(5) The child behaved badly at home. ➡ The child was badly (   ) at home.

2. 보기 A에 주어진 두 문장의 상관관계를 잘 살펴보고 이와 비슷한 패턴이 되도록 적절한 단어를 보기 B에서 골라 빈 칸을 채우시오.

Ex A

a. The students respected their professor. ➡

b. The students were respectful of their professor.

Ex B

suspicious, comprised, appreciative, envious, resentful

(1) He envied her popularity. ➡ He was (   ) of her popularity.

(2) We appreciated her kindness. ➡ We were (   ) of her kindness.

(3) Science comprises many disciplines. ➡ Science is (   ) of many disciplines.

(4) She stopped suspecting him. ➡ She stopped being (   ) of him.

(5) Some of the teammates resented the team leader's misbehavior.

➡ Some of the teammates are (   ) of the team leader's misbehavior.

3. 보기 A에 주어진 두 문장의 상관관계를 잘 살펴보고 이와 비슷한 패턴이 되도록 적절한 단어를 보기 B에서 골라 빈 칸을 채우시오.

Ex A

a. The identical twins even confused their parents. ➡
b. The identical twins were even confusing to their parents.

Ex B

intriguing, scary, disruptive, disturbing, amazing

(1) The monster scared the children. ➡ The monster was (　) to the children.

(2) His bizarre character intrigued her. ➡ His bizarre character was (　) to her.

(3) The noisy children disturbed the new English teacher.
➡ The noisy children were (　　　) to the new English teacher.

(4) The demonstration of the students disrupted the university.
➡ The demonstration of the students was (　　　) to the university

(5) David's bravery in fighting against Goliath amazed people.
➡ David's bravery in fighting against Goliath was (　　　) to people.

Coffee Break

영어에서의 외래어

영어는 인도유럽어족(Indo-European Languages)의 한 어파인 게르만어파에서 분파된 언어입니다. 한국어에 순수 국어 어휘가 아닌 외래어가 있는 것처럼 영어에도 외래어가 존재합니다. 영어의 대표적인 외래어를 살펴보겠습니다.

- kindergarten
- barbecue
- disco
- robot
- espresso
- boss

'유치원'을 의미하는 영어의 "kindergarten"은 독일어 'kindergarten'에서 유래되었습니다. 독일어에서 'kinder'는 '어린이'를 의미하며 'garten'은 '정원'을 의미합니다. '통구이'를 의미하는 영어의 'barbecue'는 스페인어 'barbecue'에서 왔습니다. 젊은이들이 즐겨 추는 'disco', 원래 영어 어휘인 것처럼 보이지만 사실은 불어 'disco'에서 온 단어입니다. 불어에서 'dancer le disco"는 '디스코를 추다'라는 표현입니다.

기계문명을 상징하는 'robot'은 오늘날 영어뿐만 아니라 다른 언어에서도 외래어로 사용되고 있습니다. 'robot'은 어느 언어에서 유래되었을까요? 'robot'은 체코작가인 Karel Capek의 희곡에 등장하는 인조인간의 이름이었습니다. 즉 원래는 고유명사였던 단어입니다. 체코어의 교유명사였던 'robot'은 영어를 포함한 다른 언어에서 외래어로 사용되기 시작하면서 '기계인간'을 의미하는 보통명사로 사용되기 시작했습니다.

영어의 'espresso'는 진한 커피의 일종입니다. 'espresso'는 원래 영어단어가 아니고 이태리어의 'esprèsso'에서 유래된 단어입니다. 이태리어에서 'esprèsso'는 '속달'이라는 의미와 '커피'의 의미를 가지고 있습니다. 한국어에서도 외래어로 사용되는 영어의 'boss'는 원래 네덜란드어의 'baas'에서 왔습니다. 이처럼 영어 어휘의 상당수가 외래어입니다. 영어에서 외래어의 존재는 영어 어휘를 풍부하게 해주는 원천이 됩니다.

Quiz. 영어의 'soldier'는 어는 언어에서 유래되었을까요?

① 독어 ② 러시아어 ③ 불어 ④ 포르투갈어

정답 : ③

Lecture 2

Basic Sentence Structure

Definition of 7 Basic Sentence Elements

Comp	Subject	Tense	Neg	(Link)	(Aspect)	Predicate

- Comp(보문어) : 문장의 유형을 나타내는 요소, 주절과 종속절을 연결하는 문장접속사
- Subject(주어) : 술어와 유기적인 의미적 관계를 갖는 요소
- Tense(시제) : 문장의 시제(과거, 현재, 미래)를 나타내는 요소
- Neg(부정어) : 문장을 부정문으로 만드는 요소
- Link(연결어) : 두 문장성분의 연결을 가능하게 하는 요소
- Aspect(상) : 진행이나 완료를 나타내는 요소
- Predicate(술어) : 의미상의 주어를 취하는 요소, 문장성분의 수와 종류를 결정하는 요소

Changeability of Parts of Speech of Predicates

- 2가 술어: Subject + (Tense) + Pred-2(Verb) + Obj

  ➡ Subject + (Tense) + Complex Pred-2(make + a + Noun + of) + Obj

(1)

The prime minister	toured	a city	on the second day.
Subj	Pred-2	Obj	Mod

(2)

He	made a tour of	noted places of the city.
Subj	Pred-2	Obj

(3)

He	decided	to drop by a gift shop.
Subj	Pred-2	Obj

(4) He / made a decision / to buy a souvenir.
Subj / Pred-2 / Obj

(5) He / did / not / choose / a luxurious item.
Subj / Tense / Neg / Pred-2 / Obj

(6) He / made a choice of / a hand-made mug.
Subj / Pred-2 / Obj

(7) He / discovered / something gripping / in the gift shop.
Subj / Pred-2 / Obj / Mod

(8) He / made a discovery of / a mysterious antique.
Subj / Pred-2 / Obj

(9) He / did / not / purchase / a fake antique.
Subj / Tense / Neg / Pred-2 / Obj

(10) He / made a purchase of / a genuine antique.
Subj / Pred-2 / Obj

- **2가 술어: Subject + (Tense) + Adv + Pred-2(V) + Obj**

  ➡ **Subject + (Tense) + Complex Pred-2(make + a + Adjective + Noun + of) + Obj**

(1) The prime minister / wisely / decided / to ride in a safe car.
Subj / Mod / Pred-2 / Obj

(2) He / made a wise decision / to ride in the bulletproof glass car.
Subj / Pred-2 / Obj

(3) His attendants (Subj) closely (Mod) inspected (Pred-2) the safety of the car (Obj).

(4) His attendants (Subj) made a close inspection of (Pred-2) the safety of the car (Obj).

(5) They (Subj) systematically (Mod) investigated (Pred-2) the possible threats (Obj).

(6) They (Subj) made a systematic investigation of (Pred-2) the causes of a possible danger (Obj).

Special Tips on Changeability of Parts of Speech of Predicates

- Compensatory Case Assigners

When the part of speech of a predicate is changed from a verb to either an adjective or a complex predicate that has a verb and a noun, compensatory prepositions such as *of* or *to* are used. In most cases the preposition *of* is used.

Ex

1. a. They respect their professors.
   b. They are respectful of their professors.
2. a. She purchased a book.
   b. She made a purchase of a book.

The reason why such prepositions are used is that neither adjective predicates nor complex predicates that are composed of a verb and a noun can assign case to their objects. Therefore, we need a compensatory preposition such as *of* to assign case to the object. For example, in the sentence *They respect their professors*, the predicate *respect* is a transitive verb that assigns accusative case to the object. However, if the predicate is changed to the adjective *respectful*, we need the preposition *of* to assign case to the object.

Ex

3. a. The identical twins even confuse their parents.
   b. The identical twins are even confusing to their parents.
4. a. The interviewer's difficult questions embarrassed the applicant.
   b. The interviewer's difficult questions were embarrassing to the applicant.

Verbs such as *confuse*, *embarrass*, *interest*, *irritate*, *surprise*, *bewilder*, and *amaze* are types of verbs with emotional meanings. When these emotional types of verbs are changed to adjectives, the preposition *to* is used to assign case. For example, in the sentence *The identical twins even confuse their parents*, the predicate *confuse* is a transitive verb that assigns accusative case to the object. However, if the predicate is changed to the adjective *confusing*, we need the preposition *to* to assign case to the object.

Dialogue 2

George: I hate rush hour traffic! We've been standing in this bus forever!

Hanna: It could be worse. We could be in a taxi.

George: What happened to Lisa anyway? I thought she was coming with you.

Hanna: She wisely decided to take the subway.

George: But she lives so far from the nearest subway station. She is going to be later than us.

(phone ring)

Hanna: That was Lisa on the phone. She's already there waiting for us.

George: What?! How can that be?

Hanna: She made a wise decision to take the subway.

Q. 위 대화문에서 나타나는 품사의 호환성은 무엇인가? (둘을 고르시오)

① 동사에서 형용사로의 변화 ② 동사에서 명사로의 변화
③ 부사에서 형용사로의 변화 ④ 형용사에서 부사로의 변화

정답 : ②, ③

Exercise 1

1. 다음 보기에 주어진 두 문장의 상관관계를 잘 살펴보고 이와 비슷한 패턴이 되도록 주어진 문장을 변화시키시오.

Ex A

a. He sings well. ➡

b. He is a good singer.

Ex B

speaker, occurrence, cook, eater, composer

(1) She cooks well. ➡ She is a good (   ).

(2) He eats heavily. ➡ He is a heavy (   ).

(3) She composes well. ➡ She is a good (   ).

(4) Blackouts occur frequently. ➡ Blackouts are a frequent (   ).

(5) John speaks English well. ➡ John is a good (   ) of English.

2. 다음 보기에 주어진 두 문장의 상관관계를 잘 살펴보고 이와 비슷한 패턴이 되도록 품사변화를 통해서 문장을 변화시키시오. (하나의 단어를 여러번 사용가능하며 필요할 경우 변형시킬 수 있음)

Ex A

a. He is planning to tour Japan for vacation. ➡

b. He is planning to make a tour of Japan for vacation.

Ex B

make, attempt, promise, appearance, plan

(1) The prisoners will attempt to escape the prison.

➡ The prisoners will (　　　) an (　　　) to escape the prison.

(2) A group of officers planned to overthrow the government.

➡ A group of officers (　　　) a (　　　) to overthrow the government.

(3) My friend promised to help me move this weekend.

➡ My friend (　　　) a (　　　) to help me move this weekend.

(4) She will appear before the audience.

➡ She will (　　　) an (　　　) before the audience.

3. 다음 보기에 주어진 두 문장의 상관관계를 잘 살펴보고 이와 비슷한 패턴이 되도록 품사변화를 통해서 문장을 변화시키시오.

Ex A

a. The detective thoroughly investigated the murder case. ➡

b. The detective made a thorough investigation of the murder case.

Ex B

wise, quick, accidental, decision, amendment, discovery

(1) She wisely decided not to buy the apartment on the top story.

➡ She will make a ( ) ( ) not to buy the apartment at the top.

(2) A scientist accidentally discovered a new scientific fact.

➡ A scientist made an ( ) ( ) of a new scientific fact.

(3) The National Assembly quickly amended the law.

➡ The National Assembly made a ( ) ( ) of the law.

Wrap Up

Changeability of Parts of Speech of Predicates

(1) 1가 술어: Subject + (Tense) + Pred-1(Verb)

➡ Subject + Tense + Pred-1(Adjective)

(2) 2가 술어: Subject + (Tense) + Pred-2(Verb) + Obj

➡ Subject + Tense + Pred-2(Adjective/of) + Obj

(3) 2가 술어: Subject + (Tense) + Pred-2(Verb) + Obj

➡ Subject + Tense + Pred-2(Adjective/to) + Obj

(4) 2가 술어: Subject + (Tense) + Pred-2(Verb) + Obj

➡ Subject + (Tense) + Complex Pred-2(make + a + Noun + of) + Obj

(5) 2가 술어: Subject + (Tense) + Adv + Pred-2(Verb) + Obj

➡ Subject + (Tense) + Complex Pred-2(make + a + Adjective + Noun + of) + Obj

Memo

UNIT 6

목적어의 분리현상

Split Object Hypothesis

Wram Up

1. 목적어의 분리 현상

- 목적어에 신체의 일부가 있는 경우 신체의 일부를 목적어에서 분리시키는 현상

Ex He kissed her hand. ➡ He kissed her on the hand.

- 전치사 사용: 목적어를 신체일부와 분리 할 때 4가지 전치사를 사용

2. 신체일부를 목적어에서 분리시킬 때 사용하는 4가지 전치사

- on ➡ 단순한 표면적 접촉
- in ➡ 강한 타격 또는 치명적 상처
- by ➡ 지속적인 접촉
- around ➡ 에워싸는 듯 한 지속적인 접촉

3. 목적어에서 신체 일부를 분리하는 예

Ex

1. a. John scratched the dog's back.
   b. John scratched the dog on the back.
2. a. She hit his eye.
   b. She hit him in the eye.
3. a. The policeman caught his hand.
   b. The policeman caught him by the hand.
4. a. I seized his waist.
   b. I seized him around the waist.

Quiz

다음 보기에 주어진 예문을 잘 살펴보고 물음에 답하시오.

Ex
1. a. John scratched the fierce dog's back.
   b. John scratched the fierce dog on the back.
2. a. The dog bit his leg.
   b. The dog bit him in the leg.
3. a. He grabbed the dog's nape.
   b. He grabbed the dog by the nape.
4. a. He seized the dog's neck.
   b. He seized the dog around the neck.

1. 위 보기에서 파란색 단어의 공통점은 무엇인가?

① 신체 일부가 내포된 목적어
② 신체의 일부가 내포된 주어
③ 신체 일부가 내포된 목적격보어
④ 신체의 일부가 내포된 수식어

2. 위 보기에서 b형 문장(1b, 2b, 3b, 4b)에 사용된 전치사의 종류는 총 몇 가지인가?

① 1가지 ② 2가지 ③ 3가지 ④ 4가지

3. 위 보기 1b와 2b에서 전치사 in을 사용하는 경우와 on을 사용하는 경우가 있다. 전치사 on을 사용하는 경우와 비교해서 전치사 in을 사용하는 경우의 특징은 무엇인가?

① 신체에 가해지는 타격이 강하거나 치명적이다.
② 신체에 가해지는 타격이 단순한 표면적 접촉이다.
③ 신체에 가해지는 타격이 순간적이다.
④ 신체에 가해지는 타격이 지속적이다.

4. 1b와 2b에서 전치사 in을 사용하는 경우와 비교해서 전치사 on을 사용하는 경우의 특징은 무엇인가?

① 신체에 가해지는 타격이 강하거나 치명적이다.

② 신체에 가해지는 타격이 단순한 표면적 접촉이다.

③ 신체에 가해지는 타격이 순간적이다.

④ 신체에 가해지는 타격이 지속적이다.

5. 보기에 주어진 문장 3b와 4b에서 전치사 by를 사용하는 경우와 around를 사용하는 경우가 있다. 전치사 by를 사용하는 경우와 around를 사용하는 경우의 공통점은 무엇인가?

① 신체에 가해지는 타격이 강하거나 치명적이다.

② 신체에 가해지는 타격이 단순한 표면적 접촉이다.

③ 신체에 가해지는 접촉이 순간적이다.

④ 신체에 가해지는 접촉이 지속성이 있다.

6. 보기에 주어진 문장 3b와 4b에서 전치사 by를 사용하는 경우와 비교해서 around를 사용하는 경우의 특징은 무엇인가?

① 원통형(round shape) 신체 일부를 둘러싸듯이 잡는다.

② 원통형(round shape) 신체일부에 가해지는 타격이 치명적이다.

③ 평면형(flat shape) 신체일부에 가해지는 접촉이 순간적이다.

④ 평면형(flat shape) 신체일부에 가해지는 접촉이 지속성이 있다.

Lecture 1

Basic Sentence Structure

Comp	Subject	Tense	Neg	Link	Aspect	Predicate

- Comp(보문어) : 문장의 유형을 나타내는 요소, 주절과 종속절을 연결하는 문장접속사
- Subject(주어) : 술어와 유기적인 의미적 관계를 갖는 요소
- Tense(시제) : 문장의 시제(과거, 현재, 미래)를 나타내는 요소
- Neg(부정어) : 문장을 부정문으로 만드는 요소
- Link(연결어) : 두 문장 성분의 연결을 가능하게 하는 요소
- Aspect(상) : 진행이나 완료를 나타내는 요소
- Predicate(술어) : 의미상의 주어를 취하는 요소, 문장성분의 수와 종류를 결정하는 요소

Split Object Hypothesis

1) Subject + Tense + Pred-2 + Obj ➡ Subject + Tense + Pred-2 + Obj + on + NP

2) Subject + Tense + Pred-2 + Obj ➡ Subject + Tense + Pred-2 + Obj + in + NP

Sentence Analysis

1) Subject + Tense + Pred-2 + Obj ➡ Subject + Tense + Pred-2 + Obj + on + NP

(1) Maria (Subj) patted (Pred-2) the dog's forehead (Obj).

(2) She	even	kissed	the dog on the forehead.
Subj	Mod	Pred-2	Obj

(3) Joshua	scratched	the dog's back.
Subj	Pred-2	Obj

(4) He	even	petted	the dog on the back.
Subj	Mod	Pred-2	Obj

(5) Maria	stroked	the dog's back.
Subj	Pred-2	Obj

(6) She	even	stroked	the dog on the neck.
Subj	Mod	Pred-2	Obj

(7) Joshua	spanked	the dog's bottom.
Subj	Pred-2	Obj

(8) He	even	pinched	the dog on the face.
Subj	Mod	Pred-2	Obj

2) Subject + Tense + Pred-2 + Obj ➡ Subject + Tense + Pred-2 + Obj + in + NP

(1) The angry dog	looked at	his face.
Subj	Pred-2	Obj

(2) The dog	even	looked	him in the eye.
Subj	Mod	Pred-2	Obj

(3) The dog	bit	his hand.
Subj	Pred-2	Obj

(4) The dog	even	bit	him in the leg.
Subj	Mod	Pred-2	Obj

(5) He	punched	the dog's head.
Subj	Pred-2	Obj

(6) He	even	punched	the dog in the face.
Subj	Mod	Pred-2	Obj

(7) He	stabbed	the dog's right side.
Subj	Pred-2	Obj

(8) He	even	stabbed	the dog in the left side.
Subj	Mod	Pred-2	Obj

(9) He	hit	the dog's stomach.
Subj	Pred-2	Pred-2

(10) He	even	hit	the dog in the eye.
Subj	Mod	Pred-2	Obj

Special Tips on Split Object Hypothesis

- **Split Object Hypothesis:**

Sometimes an object includes a part of the body. The examples include sentences such as:

> Ex
> 1. a. John kissed Mary's cheek.
>   b. She hit his eye.

In the sentence *John kissed Mary's cheek*, the object is *Mary's cheek*, and it includes a part of the body, *cheek*. In the sentence *She hit his eye*, the object is *his eye*, and it includes a part of the body, *eye*. When the object includes a part of the body, the object can be split into the pure object and the part of the body.

> Ex
> 2. a. John kissed Mary on the cheek.
>   b. She hit him in the eye.

So in the sentence *John kissed Mary's cheek*, *Mary's cheek* is split into *Mary* and *on the cheek*. The act of kissing is not a strong stroke but a slight touch on the body. We use the preposition *on* in this case. On the other hand, in the sentence *She hit his eye*, *his eye* is split into *him* and *in the eye*. The act of hitting can be a strong stroke. We use the preposition *in* in this case.

Dialogue 1

Susan: Did you hear about John and Mary's first date last night?

Jack: No, I haven't spoken to them in ages!

Susan: Well, it was going pretty well because Mary kissed John's forehead.

Jack: She kissed him on the forehead? On her first date?

Susan: Yes, but I think John took it a little further than it should have been. John kissed Mary's cheek.

Jack: Did John kiss Mary on the cheek last night? Then what happened?

Susan: Apparently she didn't like it. Mary punched John's chest.

Jack: Did she really punch John in the chest? Tell me more.

Susan: Then John hit Mary's eye.

Jack: That's nonsense. Did John really hit Mary in the eye?

Susan: Not on purpose. John was trying to defend himself.

Jack: Sounds like the worst date ever.

Susan: I agree!

Q. 위 대화문에 나타나는 목적어 분리 현상에서 전치사 in을 사용하는 동사는 무엇인가? (둘을 고르시오)

① kiss　　② punch　　③ hit　　④ hear

정답: ②, ③

Exercise 1

1. 다음 보기에 주어진 두 문장의 상관관계를 잘 이해하고 이와 유사한 패턴이 되도록 주어진 문장을 변화시키시오.

> Ex
> a. She slapped the child's back. ➡ She slapped the child on the back.
> b. The robber wounded the man's leg. ➡ The robber wounded the man in the leg.

(1) a. John patted the dog's head.
b. John patted the dog (   ) the head.

(2) a. A Hindu fanatic shot Gandhi's stomach three times.
b. A Hindu fanatic shot Gandhi (   ) the stomach three times.

(3) a. The stone hit the center of Goliath's forehead.
b. The stone hit Goliath (   ) the center of his forehead.

(4) a. She slapped the child's back.
b. She slapped the child (   ) the back.

(5) a. The robber stabbed his back.
b. The robber stabbed him (   ) the back.

(6) a. Larry tattooed Steve's chest.
b. Larry tattooed Steve (   ) the chest.

(7) a. John kissed her lips.
b. John kissed her (   ) the lips.

2. 다음에 주어진 문장들은 모두 수동태 구문이다. 따라서 주어가 능동태 구문의 목적어에 해당한다. 만약 능동태 구문에서 목적어의 분리현상이 일어난 후 수동태 구문이 만들어졌다면 어떠한 수동태 문장이 형성될까?

(1) a. The robber wounded his leg.
b. His leg was wounded by the robber.
c. The robber wounded him in the leg.
d. ( ) was wounded ( ) ( ) ( ) by the robber.

(2) a. The policeman jabbed her ribs with a club.
b. Her ribs were jabbed by the policeman with a club.
c. The policeman jabbed her in the ribs with a club.
d. ( ) was jabbed ( ) ( ) ( ) by the policeman with a club.

(3) a. He hit her eye.
b. Her eye was hit by him.
c. He hit her in the eye.
d. ( ) was hit ( ) ( ) ( ) by him.

(4) a. She stabbed his chest.
b. His chest was stabbed by her.
c. She stabbed him in the chest.
d. ( ) was stabbed ( ) ( ) ( ) by her.

(5) a. His father spanked the boy's bottom.
b. The boy's bottom was spanked by his father.
c. His father spanked the boy on the bottom.
d. ( ) ( ) was spanked ( ) ( ) ( ) by his father.

(6) a. His mom slapped the boy's back.

b. The boy's back was slapped by his mom.

c. His mom slapped the boy on the back.

d. (   ) (   ) was slapped (   ) (   ) (   ) by his mom.

Coffee Break

언어와 지역방언

미국영어와 영국영어는 서로 의사소통이 가능한 동일한 언어이지만 실제로 상당한 차이가 있다. 단적인 예로, 미국영어에서는 승강기를 "elevator"라고 하지만, 영국영어에서는 "lift"라고 하며, 미국영어에서는 바지를 "pants"라고 하지만 영국영어에서는 "trousers"라고 한다. 또 우리 한국인들이 교통수단으로 자주 이용하는 택시는 실제로 영국영어(taxi)이며, 미국영어에서는 "cab"이라고 부른다. 미국영어와 영국영어는 어휘에 있어서 이처럼 실질적인 차이가 있지만 서로 다른 언어로 분류하지 않고 같은 언어로 분류하는 이유는 의사소통이 가능하기 때문이다.

미국영어와 영국영어가 서로 어휘적 차이가 있는 것처럼 남한에서 사용되는 한국어와 북한에서 사용되는 한국어도 그렇다. 남한에서 사는 사람들은 '콘택트렌즈'를 사용하지만 북한에 사는 사람들은 '섭촉안경'을 사용한다. 남한사람들은 더운 여름날 '아이스크림'을 즐겨먹지만 북한사람들은 '얼음보숭이'를 먹는다. 또 남한사람들은 '시디플레이어'를 가지고 음악을 듣지만 북한사람들은 '레이자전축'을 이용해서 음악을 듣는다. 남한말과 북한말은 이러한 차이 외에도 많은 차이가 있다. 하지만 미국영어와 영국영어를 동일한 언어로 간주하는 것처럼 의사소통이 가능한 남한말과 북한말은 동일한 한국어로 간주된다. 동일한 언어가 사용되는 지역에 따라서 차이를 보일 경우 이를 지역 방언이라고 한다. 따라서 미국영어와 영국영어는 하나의 언어에 속하는 두 지역 방언이며, 남한말과 북한말 역시 하나의 언어로 분류되는 두 지역 방언이다.

Quiz. 남한에서 사용되는 "주스"라는 단어를 북한에서는 무엇이라고 할까요?

① 과일액체　② 과일물　③ 단물　④ 서양음료

정답 : ③

Lecture 2

Basic Sentence Structure

Comp	Subject	Tense	Neg	Link	Aspect	Predicate

- Comp(보문어) : 문장의 유형을 나타내는 요소, 주절과 종속절을 연결하는 문장접속사
- Subject(주어) : 술어와 유기적인 의미적 관계를 갖는 요소
- Tense(시제) : 문장의 시제(과거, 현재, 미래)를 나타내는 요소
- Neg(부정어) : 문장을 부정문으로 만드는 요소
- Link(연결어) : 두 문장 성분의 연결을 가능하게 하는 요소
- Aspect(상) : 진행이나 완료를 나타내는 요소
- Predicate(술어) : 의미상의 주어를 취하는 요소, 문장성분의 수와 종류를 결정하는 요소

Split Object Hypothesis

1) Subject + Tense + Pred-2 + Obj ➡ Subject + Tense + Pred-2 + Obj + by + NP

2) Subject + Tense + Pred-2 + Obj ➡ Subject + Tense + Pred-2 + Obj + around + NP

Sentence Analysis

1) Subject + Tense + Pred-2 + Obj ➡ Subject + Tense + Pred-2 + Obj + by + NP

(1) Betty	seized	her mom's hand.
Subj	Pred-2	Obj

(2) She	even	seized	her mom by the arm.
Subj	Mod	Pred-2	Obj

(3) Johnny	pulled	his dad's hair.
Subj	Pred-2	Obj

(4) He	even	pulled	him by the ear.
Subj	Mod	Pred-2	Obj

(5) Betty	grabbed	her mom's scarf.
Subj	Pred-2	Obj

(6) She	even	grabbed	her by the necklace.
Subj	Mod	Pred-2	Obj

(7) Johnny	grabbed	his collar.
Subj	Pred-2	Obj

(8) He	even	grabbed	him by the necktie.
Subj	Mod	Pred-2	Obj

(9) Johnny	held	his pet's paw.
Subj	Pred-2	Obj

(10) Betty	even	held	her pet by the tail.
Subj	Mod	Pred-2	Obj

2) Subject + Tense + Pred-2 + Obj ➡ Subject + Tense + Pred-2 + Obj + around + NP

(1) a. A cowboy (Subj) roped (Pred-2) the ox's neck. (Obj)

b. His wife (Subj) even (Mod) roped (Pred-2) the ox around the horns. (Obj)

(2) a. A rancher (Subj) rubbed (Pred-2) the horse's back. (Obj)

b. His wife (Subj) even (Mod) massaged (Pred-2) the horse around the ears. (Obj)

(3) a. A shepherd (Subj) sheared (Pred-2) the lamb's belly. (Obj)

b. His wife (Subj) sheared (Pred-2) the lamb the around the belly. (Obj)

(4) a. An animal trainer (Subj) chained (Pred-2) the dog's neck. (Obj)

b. He (Subj) even (Mod) chained (Pred-2) the lion around the neck. (Obj)

(5) a. A zoo keeper (Subj) tied (Pred-2) a troublesome monkey's hands. (Obj)

b. He (Subj) even (Mod) tied (Pred-2) him around the body. (Obj)

Special Tips on Split Object Hypothesis

Split Object Hypothesis

Sometimes an object includes a part of the body.

Ex

1. a. The child caught his mother's hand.
   b. The child held her mother's neck.

In sentence 1a the object is *his mother's hand* and it includes a part of the body, *hand*. In sentence 1b the object is *her mother's neck* and it includes a part of the body, *neck*. When the object includes a part of the body, the object can be split into the pure object and the part of the body. Examples include sentences such as:

Ex

2. a. The child caught his mother's hand.
   b. The child caught his mother by the hand.
   c. The child held her mother's neck.
   d. The child held her mother around the neck.

The act of catching is an act that lasts for a duration of time, so the preposition *by* is used when the object is split into the pure object and the part of the body. The act of holding is also an act that lasts for a duration of time. In this case the act is a case of holding something circular to surround it, so the preposition *around* is used.

Dialogue 2

Alicia: Did you know that Jenny got a job as an elementary school teacher?

Tim: I did. Did she tell you what happened in her class yesterday?

Alicia: No, she didn't. What happened?

Tim: Her students got into a fight, and Jenny tried to stop them. Her student got angry, and he pulled Jenny's hair.

Alicia: What? Did the student really pull Jenny by the hair?

Tim: Yes, and the story gets worse. Jenny tried to stop the student and she tried to tie the child's wrists.

Alicia: Did Jenny tie the child around the hands?

Tim: She didn't succeed. The student resisted and grabbed Jenny's ear.

Alicia: What? The student grabbed Jenny by the ear? How awful.

Tim: Jenny had to call his parents after the eventful day.

Alicia: I bet.

Q. 위 대화문에 나오는 동사중에서 목적어 분리현상에서 전치사 'around'를 사용하는 동사는 무엇인가?

① pull　② tie　③ resist　④ grab

정답 : ②

Exercise 1

1. 다음 보기에 주어진 두 문장의 상관관계를 잘 이해하고 이와 유사한 패턴이 되도록 주어진 문장을 변화시키시오.

> Ex He took her hand. → He took her by the hand.

(1) a. John caught her sleeve.

b. John caught ( ) ( ) ( ) ( ).

(2) a. His mother held Achilles' right ankle.

b. His mother held ( ) ( ) ( ) ( ) ( ).

(3) a. The police officer grabbed the burglar's collar.

b. The police officer grabbed ( ) ( ) ( ) ( ) ( ).

(4) a. The mischievous child pulled his mom's ear.

b. The mischievous child pulled ( ) ( ) ( ) ( ) ( ).

(5) a. She seized his hand.

b. She seized ( ) ( ) ( ) ( ).

2. 다음 보기에 주어진 예문을 잘 살펴보고 주어진 문장을 보기와 같은 패턴이 되도록 변화시키시오.

> Ex He grabbed her neck. ➡ He grabbed her around the neck.

(1) a. The cop tied the suspect's wrists.

b. The cop tied ( ) ( ) ( ) ( ) ( ).

(2) a. A cattle rancher roped the bull's horn.

b. A cattle rancher roped ( ) ( ) ( ) ( ) ( ).

(3) a. They chained Samson's legs.

b. They chained ( ) ( ) ( ) ( ).

(4) a. Two wrestlers grabbed each other's waist.

b. Two wrestlers ( ) ( ) ( ) ( ) ( ) ( ).

(5) a. A child hugged his mom's neck.

b. A child ( ) ( ) ( ) ( ) ( ) ( ).

3. 다음 쌍으로 주어진 두 문장의 의미의 차이를 기술하시오.

(1) a. Jack grabbed her by the arm.

b. Jack grabbed her around the arm.

(2) a. His mother held Achilles by the right ankle.

b. His mother held Achilles around the right ankle.

Wrap Up

Basic Sentence Structure

Comp	Subject	Tense	Neg	Link	Aspect	Predicate

- Comp(보문어) : 문장의 유형을 나타내는 요소, 주절과 종속절을 연결하는 문장접속사
- Subject(주어) : 술어와 유기적인 의미적 관계를 갖는 요소
- Tense(시제) : 문장의 시제(과거, 현재, 미래)를 나타내는 요소
- Neg(부정어) : 문장을 부정문으로 만드는 요소
- Link(연결어) : 두 문장 성분의 연결을 가능하게 하는 요소
- Aspect(상) : 진행이나 완료를 나타내는 요소
- Predicate(술어) : 의미상의 주어를 취하는 요소, 문장성분의 수와 종류를 결정하는 요소

Split Object Hypothesis

(1) 단순한 표면적 접촉

Subject + Tense + Pred-2 + Obj ➡ Subject + Tense + Pred-2 + Obj + on + NP

(2) 강한 타격 또는 치면적 상처

Subject + Tense + Pred-2 + Obj ➡ Subject + Tense + Pred-2 + Obj + in + NP

(3) 지속적인 접촉

Subject + Tense + Pred-2 + Obj ➡ Subject + Tense + Pred-2 + Obj + by + NP

(4) 에워싸는 듯한 지속적인 접촉

Subject + Tense + Pred-2 + Obj ➡ Subject + Tense + Pred-2 + Obj + around + NP

UNIT 7

주절과 종속절 1

Main Clauses and Embedded Clauses 1

Warm Up

문장을 구성하는 기본 문장 성분은 Comp, Subject, Tense, Neg, Link, Aspect, Predicate입니다. 이 중에서 가장 핵심이 되는 요소는 predicate입니다. 문장에서 predicate은 필수적인 요소로서 predicate이 있어야 문장이 형성됩니다.

문장(sentence)이 하나의 절(clause)로 되어 있는 경우를 단문(simple sentence)이라고 하고 주절(main clause)과 종속절(embedded clause)로 되어있는 문장을 복문(complex sentence)이라고 합니다. 그리고 두 개의 절이 등위접속사(and, or, but, for)로 연결되어 있는 경우를 중문(compound sentence)이라고 합니다.

1. Simple Sentence(단문)

Comp + Subject + Tense + Neg + Predicate-1

Ex Harry does not smoke.

2. Complex Sentence(복문)

Comp + Subject + Tense + Neg + Predicate-2
주절

+ Comp + Subject + Tense + Neg + Predicate
종속절

Ex Harry expects that his son will come back.

3. Compound Sentence(중문)

Comp + Subject + Tense + Neg + Predicate + and +
주절

Comp + Subject + Tense + Neg + Predicate
주절

Ex Harry won a gold medal and his brother won a bronze medal.

Quiz on Today's Lessons

1. 위 보기에 주어진 문장들은 2가 술어(predicate-2)가 주어(subject)와 목적어(object)를 취하는 예문이다. 예문에서 목적어의 품사가 2가지로 실현되고 있다. 이 2가지 품사를 고르시오.

Comp + Subject + Tense + Neg + Predicate-2 + Obj

1. Joshua talked to Susan.
2. He does not like her appearance.
3. She is losing weight.
4. He is certain that her diet will be successful.
5. How passionately he loves her!

① 명사구 ② 형용사구 ③ 부사구 ④ 절

2. 위 보기에 주어진 문장들은 2가 술어(predicate-2)가 주어(subject)와 원인(cause)을 취하는 예문이다. 원인(cause)이 될 수 있는 품사 둘을 고르시오.(to-부정사구는 절로 간주함)

Comp + Subject + Tense + Neg + Predicate-2 + Cause

1. Joshua and Susan are exhausted from their long flight.
2. They are relieved to be home safely.
3. They are happy that they are husband and wife.
4. They are excited that they are beginning their new life together.
5. They are happy that they are now free to live together.

① 전치사구 ② 형용사구 ③ 부사구 ④ 절

Comp + Subject + Tense + Neg + Pred-2 + Object

1\. a. Mina expects (주절(시제절)) that her husband will not make a mistake. (종속절(시제절))

b. Mina expects (주절(시제절)) her husband not to make a mistake. (종속절(비시제절))

2\. a. Harry hopes (주절(시세설)) that he will win a scholarship. (종속절(시제절))

b. Harry hopes (주절(시제절)) to win a scholarship. (종속절(비시제절))

3. 위 보기에 주어진 문장들은 종속절이 시제절에서 비시제절로 변화될 수 있음을 보여주고 있다. 문장 1a가 1b로 변화될 때 'to'가 들어가고 문장 2a가 2b로 변화될 때도 'to'가 들어간다. 이때 'to'의 역할은 무엇인가?

① Tense(시제) ② Neg(부정어) ③ Link(연결어) ④ Aspcct(상)

Lecture 1

Complex Sentence(복문)

- 종속절을 시제절에서 비시제절로 전환 : 주절의 주어와 종속절의 주어가 같은 경우

(1) a. Subject + Tense + Predicate-2(V) + Comp + Subject + Tense + Predicate

주절(시제절): Subject + Tense + Predicate-2(V) / 종속절(시제절): Comp + Subject + Tense + Predicate

b. Subject + Tense + Predicate-2(V) + [   ] + [   ] + [   ] + (Link) + Predicate

주절(시제절): Subject + Tense + Predicate-2(V) / 종속절(비시제절): [   ] + [   ] + [   ] + (Link) + Predicate

- 종속절을 시제절에서 비시제절로 전환 : 주절의 주어와 종속절의 주어가 다른 경우

(2) a. Subject + Tense + Neg + Predicate-2(V) + Comp + Subject + Tense + Predicate

주절(시제절): Subject + Tense + Neg + Predicate-2(V) / 종속절(시제절): Comp + Subject + Tense + Predicate

b. Subject + Tense + Neg + Predicate-2(V) + [   ] + Subj + (Link) + Predicate

주절(시제절): Subject + Tense + Neg + Predicate-2(V) / 종속절(비시제절): [   ] + Subj + (Link) + Predicate

Sentence Analysis

- embedded tensed clause → to-infinitive constructions

(1) a. Harry hopes that he will succeed in the stationery business.

주절(시제절): Harry hopes / 종속절(시제절): that he will succeed in the stationery business.

b. Harry hopes to succeed in the stationery business.

주절(시제절): Harry hopes / 종속절(비시제절): to succeed in the stationery business.

(2) a. Harry's wife expected / that she would succeed in the cosmetics business.

주절(시제절) / 종속절(시제절)

b. Harry's wife expected / to succeed in the cosmetics business.

주절(시제절) / 종속절(비시제절)

(3) a. Harry and his wife claim / that they have succeeded in their own businesses.

주절(시제절) / 종속절(시제절)

b. Harry and his wife claim / to have succeeded in their own businesses.

주절(시제절) / 종속절(비시제절)

(4) a. The children would prefer / that their parents succeed in the video game business.

주절(시제절) / 종속절(시제절)

b. The children would prefer / their parents to succeed in the video game business.

주절(시제절) / 종속절(비시제절)

(5) a. Their relatives believe / that Harry's family will be successful.

주절(시제절) / 종속절(시제절)

b. Their relatives believe / Harry's family to be successful.

주절(시제절) / 종속절(비시제절)

(6) a. They desire / that his family's business should be a great hit.

주절(시제절) / 종속절(시제절)

b. They desire / his family's business to be a great hit.

주절(시제절) / 종속절(비시제절)

- embedded tensed clause → gerund constructions

(1) a. Harry admitted (주절(시제절)) that he had made a mistake in his business. (종속절(시제절))

b. Harry admitted (주절(시제절)) having made a mistake in his business. (종속절(비시제절))

(2) a. His wife denied (주절(시제절)) that she used the wrong marketing policy. (종속절(시제절))

b. His wife denied (주절(시제절)) using the wrong marketing policy. (종속절(비시제절))

(3) a. She forgot (주절(시제절)) that she had made a wrong choice in the marketing policy. (종속절(시제절))

b. She forgot (주절(시제절)) having made a wrong choice in the marketing policy. (종속절(비시제절))

(4) a. He regrets (주절(시제절)) that he has not been careful in his business. (종속절(시제절))

b. He regrets (주절(시제절)) not having been careful in his business. (종속절(비시제절))

(5) a. I remember (주절(시제절)) that Harry and his wife have used ineffective advertisements. (종속절(시제절))

b. I remember (주절(시제절)) Harry and his wife having used ineffective advertisements. (종속절(비시제절))

(6) a. The children anticipate (주절(시제절)) that their parents' business will be a hit again. (종속절(시제절))

b. The children anticipate (주절(시제절)) their parents' business being a hit again. (종속절(비시제절))

Special Tips on Main Clause and Embedded Clauses

Sentences are usually either simple sentences or complex sentences. Simple sentences are composed of a single clause, while complex sentences are comprised of a main clause and one or more embedded clauses.

Simple Sentences

Comp + Subj + Tense + Neg + Predicate

Complex Sentences

Comp + Subj + Tense + Neg + Predicate + Comp+Subj+Tense+Neg+Predicate

(main clause: Comp + Subj + Tense + Neg + Predicate; embedded clause: Comp+Subj+Tense+Neg+Predicate)

Tense of Main Clauses and Embedded Clauses

Main clauses are almost always tensed clauses. On the other hand, the embedded clauses can be tensed clauses or tenseless clauses. When an embedded clause is a tenseless clause, the "to-infinitive" construction is usually used. However, the gerund construction is used when the predicate of the main clause is a special type of verb. These special types of verbs include verbs such as:

(1) admit	(9) *regret
(2) anticipate	(10) *forget
(3) deny	(11) *remember
(4) imagine	(12) suggest
(5) *like	(13) consider
(6) dislike	(14) advise
(7) *hate	(15) recommend
(8) *love	(16) mind

* Starred verbs can select both to-infinitive constructions and gerund constructions.

Dialogue 1

Mary: Hi Tom, I saw your brother Harry briefly yesterday. How is he doing?

Tom: He's keeping busy these days. Harry hopes that he will succeed in the stationery business.

Mary: I always knew he was ambitious. What is his goal?

Tom: The same as usual; Harry hopes to make a lot of money.

Mary: And what does the rest of his family think of all this?

Tom: Harry's kids have been very supportive of Harry and his wife's success in the business.

Mary: Really? But it's such a competitive field right now. Why Harry's wife expected to succeed in the cosmetics business is beyond me.

Tom: You know how proud they both are. In fact, Harry and his wife both claim that they have succeeded in business. But we all know the truth.

Mary: That's so sad. In this small town, everyone knows everyone else's business. I can't believe that Harry and his wife claimed to have succeeded in business when we already know the real story.

Tom: I wonder what their kids think of all this.

Mary: Well, the children would prefer for their parents to succeed in the video game business.

Tom: That would be nice. Then they could play all kinds of games for free!

Mary: Yes, but what is more important is the success of their businesses.

Tom: Sure, I wish them good luck.

Mary: Me, too.

Q. 위 대화문에서 'hope'와 'claim'이 취하는 비시제절은 어떤 종류의 비시제절 인가?

① to-부정사 구문 ② 동명사 구문 ③ 원형부정사 구문 ④ 현재분사 구문

정답 : ①

Exercise 1

아래 보기의 문장들은 종속절이 시제절에서 비시제절로 호환될 수 있음을 보여주고 있다. 보기의 예문을 잘 살펴보고 물음에 답하시오.

Ex

1. a. Harry expects (주절(시제절)) / that **he** will make a lot of money (종속절(시제절)). (Harry = he)

   b. Harry expects (주절(시제절)) / to make a lot of money (종속절(비시제절)).

2. a. Mary hopes (주절(시제절)) / that **she** will not lose money (종속절(시제절)). (Mary = she)

   b. Mary hopes (주절(시제절)) / not to lose money (종속절(비시제절)).

3. a. Harry expects (주절(시제절)) / that **she** will succeed in business (종속절(시제절)).

   b. Harry expects (주절(시제절)) / **her** to succeed in business (종속절(비시제절)).

4. a. Mary prefers (주절(시제절)) / that **he** will not leave early (종속절(시제절)).

   b. Mary prefers (주절(시제절)) / **him** not to leave early (종속절(비시제절)).

1. 종속절이 시제절에서 비시제절로 호환 될 때 종속절의 주어가 생략되는 경우도 있고 생략되지 않는 경우도 있다. 종속절의 주어가 생략되는 경우는 어떤 경우인가?

① 주절의 주어와 종속절의 주어가 같은 경우

② 주절의 주어와 종속절의 주어가 다른 경우

③ 주절의 주어와 종속절의 주어가 모두 대명사인 경우

④ 주절의 주어와 종속절의 주어가 모두 고유명사인 경우

2. 종속절이 시제절에서 비시제절로 호환 될 때 종속절의 주어가 생략되는 경우도 있고 생략되지 않는 경우도 있다. 종속절의 주어가 생략되지 않는 경우는 어떤 경우인가?

① 주절의 주어와 종속절의 주어가 같은 경우

② 주절의 주어와 종속절의 주어가 다른 경우

③ 주절의 주어와 종속절의 주어가 모두 대명사인 경우

④ 주절의 주어와 종속절의 주어가 모두 고유명사인 경우

3. 시제절의 주어와 종속절의 주어는 격(case)에 있어서 어떤 차이가 있나?

① 시제절의 주어와 비시제절의 주어 모두 주격이다.

② 시제절의 주어와 비시제절의 주어 모두 목적격이다.

③ 시제절의 주어는 주격이고 비시제절의 주어는 목적격이다.

④ 시제절의 주어는 목적격이고 비시제절의 목적어는 주격이다.

Exercise 2

아래 보기의 예문을 잘 살펴보고 물음에 답하시오.

Ex

1. a.	The children	would	prefer	that they succeed in the game business.
	Subj	Tense	Pred-2	Obj
b.	The children	would	prefer	them to succeed in the game business.
	Subj	Tense	Pred-2	Obj

2. a. Harry and his wife (Subj) claim (Pred-2) that they have not failed in their own businesses. (Obj)

b. Harry and his wife (Subj) claim (Pred-2) not to have failed in their own business. (Obj)

3. a. Harry (Subj) admitted (Pred-2) that he had made a mistake in his business. (Obj)

b. Harry (Subj) admitted (Pred-2) having made a mistake in his business. (Obj)

1. 문장 1b에서 붉은 색으로 표시된 "to"의 역할이 연결어(link)라면 "to"는 무엇과 무엇을 연결하는가?

"to"는 주절의 동사 (　　　　　　)와 종속절의 동사 (　　　　　　)를 연결한다.

2. 문장 2b에서 붉은 색으로 표시된 "to have"의 역할이 연결어(link)라면 "to have"는 무엇과 무엇을 연결하는가?

"to have"는 주절의 동사 (　　　　　　)와(과) 종속절의 동사 (　　　　　　)을(를) 연결한다.

3. 문장 3b에서 붉은 색으로 표시된 "having"의 역할이 연결어(link)라면 "having"은 무엇과 무엇을 연결하는가?

"having"은 주절의 동사 (　　　　　　)와(과) 종속절의 동사 (　　　　　　)을(를) 연결한다.

Exercise 3

아래 보기의 예문을 잘 살펴보고 물음에 답하시오.

A형 a. Sub + Tense + Pred + Comp + Subj + Tense + Pred

b. Sub + Tense + Pred + (　　) + (　　) + (　　) + Link + Pred

Ex

1. a. Harry (Subj) expects (Pred-2) that he will succeed in the stationery business (Obj).

b. Harry (Subj) expects (Pred-2) to succeed in the stationery business (Obj).

B형 a. Sub + Tense + Pred + Comp + Subj + Tense + Pred

b. Sub + Tense + Pred + (　　) + (　　) + (　　) + (Link) + Pred

Ex

1. a. Sue (Subj) remembers (Pred-2) that she met her once (Obj).

b. Sue (Subj) remembers (Pred-2) meeting her once (Obj).

1. 위 보기에 주어진 예문은 종속절의 시제절에서 비시제절로의 호환성을 보여준다. 종속절이 시제절에서 비시제절로 호환 될 때 A형처럼 "to-부정사"를 사용하는 경우와 문장 B형처럼 동명사를 사용하는 경우가 있다. A형과 B형을 결정하는 것은 주절의 술어동사에 달려있다. 다음 주어진 동사가 A형과 B형 중에서 어느 형에 해당하는 지 명시하시오.

(1) admit (인정하다)

(2) expect (기대하다)

(3) hope (희망하다)

(4) desire (바라다)

(5) anticipate (예상하다)

(6) deny (부인하다)

(7) imagine (상상하다)

(8) like/love (평소에 ~하는 것을 좋아하다)

(9) like/love (지금 ~하는 것을 원하다 / would + V + 목적어)

(10) dislike (싫어하다)

(11) claim (주장하다)

(12) regret (~했던 것을 후회하다)

(13) regret (~해야 하는 것을 유감스럽게 생각하다)

(14) forget (~했던 것을 잊다)

(15) forget (~할 것을 잊다)

(16) remember (~했던 것을 기억하다)

(17) remember (~할 것을 기억하다)

(18) suggest (제안하다)

(19) consider (고려하다)

(20) mind (꺼려하다)

(21) agree (동의하다)

Exercise 4

1. 다음 보기에 주어진 종속절을 비시절로 바꾸시오.

(1) a. Mr. Smith agreed that he would share his office with visiting professors.

b. Mr. Smith agreed ( ) ( ) his office with visiting professors.

(2) a. Mrs. Smith admitted that she had not cooked dinner for his family.

b. Mrs. Smith admitted ( ) ( ) cooked dinner for his family.

(3) a. Maria has always regretted that she sold the farm.

b. Maria has always regretted ( ) the farm.

(4) a. We regret that we must say that you owe the bank two million won.

b. We regret ( ) ( ) that you owe the bank two million won.

(5) a. Please remember that you should lock the door when you leave.

b. Please remember ( ) ( ) the door when you leave.

(6) a. Judy remembers that she had been scolded by her parents.

b. Judy remembers ( ) ( ) scolded by her parents.

Fortune telling in the west

In western countries, which have developed a scientific worldview based upon rational thought, fortune telling and other forms of divination are not as common as they are in other parts of the world. However, that does not mean that they do not exist. Perhaps because they represent old folk customs that still linger, or perhaps because western people are not as strictly rational as they like to believe they are, various forms of fortune telling still exist in the West today.

If you open a newspaper in most English-speaking countries, you will often find an astrology column inside. Astrology is the belief that you can tell a person's future fate by examining a person's 'horoscope' - a special chart that an astrologer makes by plotting the positions of certain planets in the sky when the person is born. Whether or not people truly take such predictions seriously is open to doubt. Usually the predictions in a newspaper's astrology column are so vague that they could be true for almost anybody.

Another type of divination or fortune telling that is occasionally practised in the West is palm reading. This is the belief that you can find information about a person's character and future prospects by examining the lines on his or her palm. Traditionally, this was an art practised by travelling gypsies, who would set up a tent at a village fair and would tell fortunes to all who would "cross their palms with silver", i.e. pay for a palm reading.

Alongside these methods for telling the future, there are a number of common superstitions in the West which some people believe have an effect on a person's luck. In particular, the number 13 is considered unlucky in English-speaking countries, much in the same way that '4' is considered unlucky in East Asia. Friday the thirteenth in any month is believed by some to be a particularly unlucky date.

It seems that fortune-telling and superstition are among the most ancient ways in which human beings have tried to influence the world and understand their place in it.

Quiz. What number is considered to be a lucky number in Korean culture?

① four ② five ③ six ④ seven

정답 : ④

Lecture 2

Complex Sentence(복문)

- 종속절을 시제절에서 비시제절로 전환 : 주절의 술어가 형용사인 경우
  (주절의 주어=종속절의 주어)

(1) a. Subject + Tense + Predicate-2(Adj) +
주절(시제절)

Comp + Subject + Tense + Neg + Pred-2 + Obj
종속절(시제절)

b. Subject + Tense + Predicate-2(Adj) +
주절(시제절)

[ ] + [ ] + [ ] + Neg + Link + Pred-2 + Obj
종속절(비시제절)

Sentence Analysis

(1) a. Steve is sorry (주절(시제절)) that he cannot use the internet on his mobile phone. (종속절(시제절))

b. He is upset (주절(시제절)) not to be able to check emails on his mobile phone. (종속절(비시제절))

(2) a. Tina is disappointed (주절(시제절)) that she cannot download games on her feature phone. (종속절(시제절))

b. She is deeply disappointed (주절(시제절)) not to be able to use Kakao Talk on her feature phone. (종속절(비시제절))

(3) a. Steve and Tina are upset / that they cannot use navigation systems on their feature phones.

주절(시제절) / 종속절(시제절)

b. They are depressed / not to be able to search for information on their feature phones.

주절(시제절) / 종속절(비시제절)

(4) a. Steve and Tina are happy / that they got free smartphones.

주절(시제절) / 종속절(시제절)

b. He is overjoyed / to download the latest version of Kakao Talk on his smartphone.

주절(시제절) / 종속절(비시제절)

(5) a. He is happy / that he can use Kakao Talk to communicate with his friends.

주절(시제절) / 종속절(시제절)

b. He is delighted / to be able to take courses on his new smartphone.

주절(시제절) / 종속절(비시제절)

(6) a. He is delighted / to be able to use navigation systems on his smartphone.

주절(시제절) / 종속절(시제절)

b. She is excited / to download new games on her new smartphone.

주절(시제절) / 종속절(비시제절)

(7) a. Steven and Tina are amazed / that they can perform multiple tasks on their smartphones.

주절(시제절) / 종속절(시제절)

b. They are overjoyed / to be able to use their smartphones 24 hours a day.

주절(시제절) / 종속절(비시제절)

(8) a. They are happy	that they can do almost everything on their smartphones.
주절(시제절)	종속절(시제절)

b. They are happy	to carry their smartphones wherever they go.
주절(시제절)	종속절(비시제절)

Special Tips on Cause and Object

Two-place predicates require two syntactic elements. Adjectives of emotion are predicates that require a subject and a cause. Adjectives of emotion include words such as "sorry," "disappointed," "upset," "surprised," "happy," "angry," "glad," "amazed," and "embarrassed". These adjectives require a subject and a cause. The difference between a cause and an object is that the cause can be represented either by a *that*-clause or a *because*-clause, whereas an object is represented by a *that*-clause alone.

1. a. James	is	sure	that he will win a scholarship. (○)
Subj	Tense	Pred-2	Obj

b. John	is	sure	because he will win a scholarship. (×)
Subj	Tense	Pred-2	Obj

2. a. Marina	is	happy	that she won a scholarship. (○)
Subj	Tense	Pred-2	Cause

b. Marina	is	happy	because she won a scholarship. (○)
Subj	Tense	Pred-2	Cause

Dialogue 2

Mary: I'm so glad that we got smartphones for our children.

Bill: I know. Me, too.

Mary: We waited so long for financial reasons, but now I think it's totally worth it since we will always be able to reach our kids.

Bill: I feel the same. The kids seem pretty pleased about having smartphones as well, except that Tina is disappointed that she cannot play games on her cell phone.

Mary: Well, that's not what the phone is for, anyway.

Bill: Yeah, if she has free time, she needs to study.

Mary: That's true. And at least Tina is excited that she can video chat with Steve on her new smartphone.

Bill: Yeah, I think she plans to do it for the first time on Thursday. She told me she is excited to video chat with Steve on her new smartphone.

Mary: That's good. Now we just need to get them to download some apps for studying with their smartphones.

Bill: Great idea!

Q. 위 대화문에서 종속절에서 시제절과 to-부정사 구문(비시제절)의 호환을 보이는 주절의 술어는 무엇인가?

① glad　② pleased　③ excited　④ need

정답 : ③

Exercise 1

- Fill in the blanks with the apprapriate words.

(1) a. Bill is sorry that he is late to class.

b. Bill is sorry (   ) (   ) late to class.

(2) a. Angelina is happy that she has someone to talk with.

b. Angelina is happy (   ) (   ) someone to talk with.

(3) a. Scott was disappointed that he lost the game.

b. Scott was disappointed (   ) (   ) the game.

(4) a. Jina was upset that she had failed the exam.

b. Jina was upset (   ) (   ) (   ) the exam.

(5) a. Tina is disappointed that she scored only two points in the game.

b. Tina is disappointed (   ) (   ) (   ) only two points in the game.

(6) a. Scott and Lydia are amazed that they found such great jobs.

b. Scott and Lydia are amazed (   ) (   ) (   ) such great jobs.

Wrap Up

● 종속절을 시제절에서 비시제절로 전환

(1) 주절의 주어와 종속절의 주어가 같은 경우

a. Subject + Tense + Predicate-2(V) + Comp + Subject + Tense + Neg + Predicate

주절(시제절)	종속절(시제절)
Subject + Tense + Predicate-2(V)	Comp + Subject + Tense + Neg + Predicate

b. Subject + Tense + Predicate-2(V) + [ ] + [ ] + [ ] + Neg + (Link) + Predicate

주절(시제절)	종속절(비시제절)
Subject + Tense + Predicate-2(V)	[ ] + [ ] + [ ] + Neg + (Link) + Predicate

(2) 주절의 주어와 종속절의 주어가 다른 경우

a. Subject + Tense + Neg + Predicate-2(V) + Comp + Subject + Tense + Predicate

주절(시제절)	종속절(시제절)
Subject + Tense + Neg + Predicate-2(V)	Comp + Subject + Tense + Predicate

b. Subject + Tense + Neg + Predicate-2(V) + [ ] + Subj + [ ] + (Link) + Predicate

주절(시제절)	종속절(비시제절)
Subject + Tense + Neg + Predicate-2(V)	[ ] + Subj + [ ] + (Link) + Predicate

(3) 주절의 술어가 형용사인 경우(주절의 주어와 종속절의 주어가 같은 경우)

a. Subject + Tense + Predicate-2(Adj) + Comp + Subject + Tense + Neg + Predicate

주절(시제절)	종속절(시제절)
Subject + Tense + Predicate-2(Adj)	Comp + Subject + Tense + Neg + Predicate

b. Subject + Tense + Predicate-2(Adj) + [ ] + [ ] + [ ] + Neg + Link + Predicate

주절(시제절)	종속절(비시제절)
Subject + Tense + Predicate-2(Adj)	[ ] + [ ] + [ ] + Neg + Link + Predicate

GRAMMAR DNA 총정리 연습문제

UNIT 1~7

PART 1. 다음 주어진 지문을 읽고 물음에 답하시오.

> Ex　Comp　Subject　[①]　Neg　[②]　[③]　Predicate

1. 보기의 빈 칸에 들어갈 문장 성분을 순서대로 가장 적절히 배열한 것은?

① Link, Aspect, Tense　　② Tense, Aspect, Link
③ Tense, Link, Aspect　　④ Aspect, Link, Tense

2. 진행(progressive state)이나 완료(perfective state)를 나타내는 문장 성분은?

① Tense　② Neg　③ Link　④ Aspect

3. 두 문장 성분의 연결을 가능하게 하는 요소는?

① Tense　② Neg　③ Link　④ Aspect

4. 보기 주어진 문장에서 빈도부사의 위치를 가장 잘 설명한 것은?

> Ex　The boy will not often be scolded.

① Neg와 Predicate 사이에 위치한다.　　② Tense와 Neg 사이에 위치한다.
③ Neg와 Predicate 사이에 위치한다.　　④ Neg와 Link 사이에 위치한다.

보기에 주어진 문장을 보고 물음에 답하시오.

Ex

a. He is overweight.
b. She was blamed for the mistake.
c. He has come back.
d. She exercises on a regular basis.
e. He is scolding her.

5. 위 보기에 주어진 문장 중에서 술어가 시제를 가지고 있는 문장은?

① 문장 a ② 문장 b ③ 문장 c ④ 문장 d ⑤ 문장 e

6. 위 보기에 주어진 문장 중에서 술어가 수동형 과거분사인 경우는?

① 문장 a ② 문장 b ③ 문장 c ④ 문장 d ⑤ 문장 e

PART 2. 다음 주어진 지문을 읽고 물음에 답하시오.

Ex

a. It is possible that Sue will pass the exam.
b. It is probable that Sue will pass the exam.
c. It is surprising that Sue passed the exam.
d. It is likely that Sue will pass the exam.

7. 위 보기에 주어진 문장들 중에서 종속절의 주어가 주절 주어로 이동할 수 있는 문장은?

① 문장 a ② 문장 b ③ 문장 c ④ 문장 d

Ex Sue is (①) (②) pass the exam.

8. 위 보기에 주어진 문장들 중 한 문장에서 종속절의 주어가 실제로 주절 주어로 이동하면 보기와 같은 문장이 형성된다. 빈 칸에 들어갈 두 단어를 쓰시오.

① ____________ ② ____________

Ex prove, certain, happen, unlikely, turn out, seem

9. 위 보기에 주어진 술어의 공통점은 무엇인가?

① 주어를 취하는 1가 술어 ② 명제를 취하는 1가 술어
③ 주어와 원인을 취하는 2가 술어 ④ 주어와 목적어를 취하는 2가 술어

Ex easy, impossible, difficult, possible, hard, probable

10. 위 보기에 주어진 술어의 공통점은 무엇인가?

① 주어를 취하는 1가 술어 ② 명제를 취하는 1가 술어
③ 주어와 원인을 취하는 2가 술어 ④ 주어와 목적어를 취하는 2가 술어

Ex
a. It happened that he saw her yesterday. (a = b)
b. He happened (①) (②) her yesterday.
c. It is certain that he divorced his wife. (c = d)
d. He is certain (③) (④) divorced his wife.

11. 위 보기의 빈 칸 ①, ②에 들어갈 적절한 표현을 쓰시오.

① ______________________ ② ______________________

12. 위 보기의 빈 칸 ③, ④에 들어갈 적절한 표현을 쓰시오.

③ ______________________ ④ ______________________

PART 3. 다음 주어진 문장들이 보기에 어떤 유형의 문장인지 고르시오. (보기에 주어진 문장의 유형은 한 번 이상 선택될 수 있음)

Ex

a. Subj + Tense + Predicate-2 + Subject Complement
b. Subj + Tense + Predicate-2 + Object
c. Subj + Tense + Predicate-2 + Location
d. Subj + Tense + Predicate-2 + Substance
e. Subj + Tense + Predicate-2 + Cause

13. We are opposed to the building of the new road. ( )

14. He weighs 160 pounds. ( )

15. CUFS is located in Seoul. ( )

16. The classroom is full of students. ( )

17. Jimmy was surprised that he passed the exam. ( )

18. I am sure that he will succeed in his new business. ( )

PART 4. 다음 주어진 지문을 읽고 물음에 답하시오.

> **Ex** promise, persuade, tell, ask, rob, prevent, keep from, inform

19. 위 보기에 주어진 술어들이 공통으로 형성할 수 있는 문장의 유형은?

① Subj + Tense + Predicate−3 + DO + IO

② Subj + Tense + Predicate−3 + IO + DO

③ Subj + Tense + Predicate−3 + Obj + Source

④ Subj + Tense + Predicate−3 + Obj + Location

> **Ex** blame, scold, censure, criticize, praise, reward, thank

20. 위 보기에 주어진 술어들이 공통으로 형성할 수 있는 문장의 유형은?

① Subj + Tense + Predicate−3 + Obj + Substance

② Subj + Tense + Predicate−3 + Obj + Cause

③ Subj + Tense + Predicate−3 + Obj + Object Complement

④ Subj + Tense + Predicate−3 + Obj + Source

다음 주어진 문장들이 보기에 어떤 유형의 문장인지 고르시오.
(보기에 주어진 문장의 유형 중 하나는 선택되지 않음)

> **Ex**
> a. Subj + Tense + Predicate-3 + DO + IO
> b. Subj + Tense + Predicate-3 + IO + DO
> c. Subj + Tense + Predicate-3 + Object + Object Complement
> d. Subj + Tense + Predicate-3 + Object + Location
> e. Subj + Tense + Predicate-3 + Object + Source

21. He will supply the school with new desks and chairs. ( )

22. The students will also receive financial aid from him. ( )

23. The university will place a commemorative statue of him in front of the library. ( )

24. They think of him as a mentor. ( )

PART 5. 주어진 문장a와 문장b가 동일한 의미의 문장이 되기 위해서 빈 칸에 들어갈 적절한 단어를 보기에서 선택하여 쓰시오. (보기에 주어진 문장의 유형은 한 번 이상 선택될 수 있음)

Ex

successful, suspicious, appreciative, resentful, scary, tour, made, cook, good, of, to, being, is, are, was

25. a. She finally succeeded in bringing rain.
    b. She was finally ( ) in bringing rain.

26. a. She stopped suspecting him.
    b. She stopped being ( ) ( ) him.

27. a. He appreciates her kindness.
    b. He ( ) ( ) ( ) her kindness.

28. a. We toured Italy for a week.
    b. We ( ) a ( ) ( ) Italy for a week.

29. a. The monster scared the children.

b. The monster (   ) (   ) (   ) the children.

30. a. She cooks well.

b. She is a (   ) (   ).

PART 6. 주어진 문장a와 문장b가 동일한 의미의 문장이 되기 위해서 빈 칸에 들어갈 적절한 단어를 보기에서 선택하여 쓰시오. (보기에 주어진 문장의 유형은 한 번 이상 선택될 수 있음)

Ex   on, in, by, around

31. a. She slapped the child's back.

b. She slapped the child (   ) the back.

32. a. A Hindu fanatic shot Gandhi's stomach three times.

b. A Hindu fanatic shot Gandhi (   ) the stomach three times.

33. a. The robber wounded his leg.

b. He was wounded (   ) the leg.

34. a. His father spanked the boy's bottom.

b. The boy was spanked (   ) the bottom by his father.

35. a. His mother held Achilles' right ankle.

b. His mother held Achilles (   ) the right ankle.

36. a. A child hugged his mom's neck.

b. A child hugged his mom (   ) the neck.

PART 7. 주어진 문장a와 문장b가 동일한 의미의 문장이 되기 위해서 빈 칸에 들어갈 적절한 단어를 써넣으시오.

37. a. They are happy that they live together.

b. They are happy (   ) (   ) together.

38. a. Mina expects that her husband will not make a mistake.

b. Mina expects her husband (   ) (   ) make a mistake.

39. a. Harry admitted that he had made a mistake in his business.

b. Harry admitted (   ) made a mistake in his business.

40. a. Judy remembers that she had been scolded by her parents.

b. Judy remembers (   ) (   ) scolded by her parents.

UNIT 9 주절과 종속절 2

Main Clauses and Embedded Clauses 2

Warm Up

문장을 구성하는 문장 성분은 Comp, Subject, Tense, Neg, Link, Aspect, Predicate 입니다. 이 중에서 가장 핵심이 되는 요소는 predicate입니다. 문장이 단문(simple sentence)으로 되어 있는 경우는 Comp, Subject, Tense, Neg, Link, Aspect, Predicate이 한 번 등장하며 복문(complex sentence)으로 되어있는 경우는 Comp, Subject, Tense, Neg, Link, Aspect, Predicate이 두 번 이상 등장합니다.

문장이 주절(main clause)과 종속절(embedded clause)로 되어 있는 경우 종속절은 문장의 목적어(object) 또는 원인(cause)이 될 수도 있으며 또 주절을 수식하는 수식어(modifier)가 될 수도 있습니다. 본 단원에서는 수식어 역할을 하는 종속절을 시제절에서 비시제절로 변화시키는 과정을 학습하도록 하겠습니다.

1. Types of Complex Sentences

(1) Comp + Subject + Tense + Neg + Predicate + Comp + Subject + Tense + Neg + Predicate

주절 / 종속절(목적어)

(2) Comp + Subject + Tense + Neg + Predicate + Comp + Subject + Tense + Neg + Predicate

주절 / 종속절(원인)

(3) Comp + Subject + Tense + Neg + Predicate + Comp + Subject + Tense + Neg + Predicate

주절 / 종속절(수식어)

Quiz on Today's Lessons

Ex

1. I will lend you my car (주절) if you don't have one. (종속절)

2. I can't go out with you (주절) because I am working this evening. (종속절)

3. Although he was helpful, (종속절) he was not much liked. (주절)

4. When she was questioned, (종속절) she denied having told him a lie. (주절)

5. While I was walking along the street, (종속절) I met one of my high school friends. (주절)

1. 종속절이 양보(concession)의 의미를 가지고 있는 문장은 어떤 문장인가?

① 1번 문장 ② 2번 문장 ③ 3번 문장 ④ 4번 문장 ⑤ 5번 문장

2. 종속절이 동시상황(simultaneous temporal situation)의 의미를 가지고 있는 문장은 어떤 문장인가?

① 1번 문장 ② 2번 문장 ③ 3번 문장 ④ 4번 문장 ⑤ 5번 문장

3. 종속절이 시점(point in time)을 나태는 문장은 어떤 문장인가?

① 1번 문장 ② 2번 문장 ③ 3번 문장 ④ 4번 문장 ⑤ 5번 문장

4. 종속절이 이유(reason)를 나타내는 문장은 어떤 문장인가?

① 1번 문장 ② 2번 문장 ③ 3번 문장 ④ 4번 문장 ⑤ 5번 문장

5. 종속절이 조건(condition)을 나타내는 문장은 어떤 문장인가?

① 1번 문장 ② 2번 문장 ③ 3번 문장 ④ 4번 문장 ⑤ 5번 문장

Lecture 1

시제절과 비시제절의 호환성

● 복문에서 수식어인 종속절을 시제절에서 비시제절로 바꾸기

· 주절의 주어와 종속절의 주어가 같은 경우

(1) a. Subject + Tense + Neg + Predicate (주절(시제절)) + Comp + Subject + Tense + Predicate (종속절(시제절))

b. Subject + Tense + Neg + Predicate (주절(시제절)) + Comp + Φ + Φ + (Link) + Predicate (종속절(비시제절))

● 수식어인 종속절을 시제절에서 비시제절로 바꾸는 과정

· 종속절의 Comp ➡ 필요에 따라서 생략(because, since, as, if)

· 종속절의 주어 ➡ 생략

· 종속절의 동사(Tense, Predicate) ➡ Verb-ing(현재분사)

Ex 1. a. You should be careful (주절(시제절)) when you deal with poisonous animals (종속설(시제절)).

b. You should be careful (주절(시제절)) when dealing with poisonous animals (종속절(비시제절)).

Ex 2. a. Because he is very cooperative, (종속절(시제절)) he is popular with his coworkers (주절(시제절)).

b. Being very cooperative, (종속절(비시제절)) he is popular with his coworkers (주절(시제절)).

Sentence Analysis

(1) a. When he reached the age of 30, / he received an inheritance from his parents.
종속절(시제절) / 주절(시제절)

b. When reaching the age of 30, / he received an inheritance from his parents.
종속절(비시제절) / 주절(시제절)

(2) a. Though he did not have a successful plan, / he left his parents to find his own fortune.
종속절(시제절) / 주절(시제절)

b. Though not having a successful plan, / he left his parents to find his own fortune.
종속절(비시제절) / 주절(시제절)

(3) a. Since he left his parents, / he has led a wild life.
종속절(시제절) / 주절(시제절)

b. Since leaving his parents, / he has led a wild life.
종속절(비시제절) / 주절(시제절)

(4) a. When he traveled abroad, / he squandered all his fortune.
종속절(시제절) / 주절(시제절)

b. When traveling abroad, / he squandered all his fortune.
종속절(비시제절) / 주절(시제절)

(5) a. After he had lost all his money, / he began to miss his parents.
종속절(시제절) / 주절(시제절)

b. After having lost all his money, / he began to miss his parents.
종속절(비시제절) / 주절(시제절)

(6) a. While he was returning to his hometown, he tripped over a stone.

종속절(시제절) 주절(시제절)

b. While returning to his hometown, he tripped over a stone.

종속절(비시제절) 주절(시제절)

(7) a. Even before he reached his parents' house, he was nervous.

종속절(시제절) 주절(시제절)

b. Even before reaching his parents' house, he was nervous.

종속절(비시제절) 주절(시제절)

(8) a. Because he was completely bankrupt, he was ashamed of himself.

종속절(시제절) 주절(시제절)

b. Being completely bankrupt, he was ashamed of himself.

종속절(비시제절) 주절(시제절)

(9) a. When he was given new clothing, he began to sob.

종속절(시제절) 주절(시제절)

b. When (being) given new clothing, he began to sob.

종속절(비시제절) 주절(시제절)

Special Tips on Interchangeability between Tensed and Tenseless Clauses for the Embedded Clauses.

Complex sentences are comprised of a main clause and an embedded clause. The main clauses are almost always tensed clauses; however, the embedded clauses are either tensed clauses or tenseless clauses.

- The Tense of Clauses

  Comp + Subject + Tense + Neg + Predicate +
  main clause(tensed clause)

  Comp + Subject + Tense + Neg + Predicate
  embedded clause(tensed or tenseless clause)

- The Types of Tenseless Embedded Clauses

  (1) object embedded clause

  · to-infinitive constructions

Ex

a. John expects (tensed MC) that his son will enter Harvard University (tensed EC).

b. John expects (tensed MC) his son to enter Harvard University (tenseless EC).

· gerund constructions

a. John regrets that he has spent all of his inheritance.
tensed MC — tensed EC

b. John regrets having spent all of his inheritance.
tensed MC — tenseless EC

· bare infinitive construction

a. Sue saw that her husband opened the door.
tensed MC — tensed EC

b. Sue saw her husband open the door.
tensed MC — tenseless EC

· present participle constructions

a. John witnessed that his son was being scolded by a woman.
tensed MC — tensed EC

b. John witnessed his son being scolded by a woman.
tensed MC — tenseless EC

(2) modifier embedded clause

· present participle constructions

Ex a. You should not monopolize the conversation when you talk with your seniors.
tensed MC — tensed EC

b. You should not monopolize the conversation when talking with your seniors.
tensed MC — tenseless EC

· past participle constructions

Ex a. The child stopped crying when he was given something to eat.
tensed MC — tensed EC

b. The child stopped crying when (being) given something to eat.
tensed MC — tenseless EC

c. She began to cry when she was scolded.
tensed MC — tensed EC

d. She began to cry when (being) scolded.
tensed MC — tenseless EC

Dialogue 1

Paul : Hi, honey. Did you notice the child not wearing socks outside?

Sue : Why yes, darling. I did notice that the child was not wearing socks.

Paul : That's pretty funny, isn't it?

Sue : Yes, sweetie-pie. It's hilarious.

Paul : Haha…. Oh no! I just realized that when buying spaghetti at the supermarket, I forgot the sauce.

Sue : When you bought spaghetti, you forgot the sauce? Oh, honey! Why are you always so forgetful?

Paul : I don't know, dear. I guess it just comes with the package.

Sue : Since getting to know you, I've really come to appreciate that package.

Paul : Oh, that's so sweet, my darling dear. Since I got to know you, I've come to appreciate your package, too.

Sue : Oh, aren't we just the sweetest couple?

Q. 위 대화문에서 종속절에서 비시제절과 시제절의 호환을 보이는 주절의 술어는 무엇인가?

① notice ② realize ③ appreciate ④ know

정답 : ①

Exercise 1

다음 주어진 예문을 살펴보고 물음에 답하시오.

1\. a. John expects (주절(시제절)) | that his son will enter Harvard University. (종속절(시제절))

b. John expects (주절(시제절)) | his son to enter Harvard University. (종속절(to 부정사 구문))

2\. a. John regrets (주절(시제절)) | that he has spent all of his inheritance. (종속절(시제절))

b. John regrets (주절(시제절)) | having spent all of his inheritance. (종속절(동명사 구문))

3\. a. Sue saw (주절(시제절)) | that her husband opened the door. (종속절(시제절))

b. Sue saw (주절(시제절)) | her husband open the door. (종속절(원형부정사 구문))

4\. a. John witnessed (주절(시제절)) | that his son was being scolded by a woman. (종속절(시제절))

b. John witnessed (주절(시제절)) | his son being scolded by a woman. (종속절(현재분사 구문))

주절(main clause)과 종속절(embedded clause)로 되어 있는 복문(complex sentence)에서 종속절은 목적어(object), 원인(cause), 또는 수식어(modifier) 역할을 할 수 있다. 목적어 역할을 하는 종속절은 비시제 절에서 4가지 유형으로 나타난다. 4가지 유형은 다음과 같다.

1. to-부정사 구문(to-infinitive construction)
2. 원형부정사 구문(bare infinitive construction)
3. 동명사 구문(gerund construction)
4. 현재분사 구문(present participle construction)

1. 위 4가지 유형의 비시제절 중에서 종속절에 현재분사 구문(present participle construction)을 사용하는 경우는 어떤 경우인가?

① 진행을 나타내는 경우

② 주절의 술어가 지각동사(verb of perception)인 경우

③ 완료를 나타내는 경우

④ 주절의 술어가 특정동사(admit, anticipate, deny, imagine, suggest, etc)인 경우나 전치사인 경우

2. 위 4가지 유형의 비시제절 중에서 종속절에 동명사 구문(gerund construction)을 사용하는 경우는 어떤 경우인가?

① 진행을 나타내는 경우

② 주절의 술어가 지각동사(verbs of perception)인 경우

③ 완료를 나타내는 경우

④ 주절의 술어가 특정동사(admit, anticipate, deny, imagine, suggest, etc)인 경우나 전치사인 경우

3. 위 4가지 유형의 비시제절 중에서 종속절에 원형부정사 구문(bare infinitive construction)을 사용하는 경우는 어떤 경우인가?

① 진행을 나타내는 경우
② 주절의 술어가 지각동사(verb of perception)인 경우
③ 완료를 나타내는 경우
④ 주절의 술어가 특정동사(admit, anticipate, deny, imagine, suggest, etc)인 경우나 전치사인 경우

4. 위 4가지 유형의 비시제절 중에서 종속절에 to-부정사 구문(to-infinitive construction)을 사용하는 경우는 어떤 경우인가?

① 진행을 나타내는 경우
② 주절의 술어가 지각동사(verb of perception)인 경우
③ 주절의 술어가 특정동사(admit, anticipate, deny, imagine, suggest, etc)인 경우나 전치사인 경우
④ ①번, ②번, ③번을 제외 한 나머지 경우

Exercise 2

다음 주어진 예문을 살펴보고 물음에 답하시오.

Ex

1. a. You should not monopolize the conversation (주절(시제절)) when you talk with your seniors. (종속절(시제절))

   b. You should not monopolize the conversation (주절(시제절)) when talking with your seniors. (종속절(비시제절))

2. a. John met his ex-girlfriend (주절(시제절)) while he was walking to school. (종속절(시제절))

   b. John met his ex-girlfriend (주절(시제절)) while walking to school. (종속절(비시제절))

3. a. The child stopped crying (주절(시제절)) when he was given something to eat. (종속절(시제절))

   b. The child stopped crying (주절(시제절)) when (being) given something to eat. (종속절(비시제절))

4. a. She began to cry (주절(시제절)) when she was scolded. (종속절(시제절))

   b. She began to cry (주절(시제절)) when (being) scolded. (종속절(비시제절))

1. 주절과 종속절로 되어 있는 복문에서 종속절은 시제절과 비시제절이 모두 가능하다. 비시제절의 유형은 to-부정사 구문(to-infinitive construction), 원형부정사 구문(bare infinitive construction), 동명사 구문(gerund construction), 또는 현재분사 구문(present participle construction)이 있다. 위 보기의 b형 문장은 비시제절로서 모두 현재분사 구문이다. b형 문장의 종속절이 가지고 있는 공통점은 무엇인가?

   ① 진행　　② 완료　　③ 수동　　④ 부사절

2. 다음 주어진 예문의 종속절을 시제절에서 비시제절로 바꾸시오.

① a. When she turned the corner, she sprained her ankle.

b. ______________________, she sprained her ankle.

② a. Since I entered university, my tastes have changed.

b. ______________________, my tastes have changed.

③ a. Though I wore a coat, I was still cold.

b. __________________, I was still cold.

④ a. While I was running for the bus, I tripped over a stone.

b. ___________________________, I tripped over a stone.

⑤ a. After he had graduated from college, he went abroad to get a job.

b. ______________________________, he went abroad to get a job.

⑥ a. Before I went to the USA, I had never eaten a hamburger.

b. ______________________, I had never eaten a hamburger.

⑦ a. Because she had no money, she could not afford to buy a car.

b. ______________________, she could not afford to buy a car.

3. 보문어(complementizer)는 주절과 종속절을 연결하는 문장접속사 역할을 할 수 도 있고 문장의 유형을 명시하는 역할을 할 수도 있다. 시제절에서 사용되는 보문어는 비시제절에서 생략될 수도 있고 생략되지 않을 수도 있다. 다음에 주어진 보문어 중에서 비시제절에서 언제나 반드시 생략되어야 하는 보문어 넷을 고르시오.

① when ② while ③ though ④ since(~이래로) ⑤ since(~때문에)
⑥ because ⑦ after ⑧ before ⑨ while ⑩ as ⑪ if

Coffee Break

언어와 음조(language and tone)

지구상에는 한국어(Korean), 영어(English), 중국어(Chinese), 일본어(Japanese), 불어(French), 러시아어(Russian)와 같은 많은 언어가 존재합니다. 모든 언어에는 '음조'(intonation)가 있습니다. 음조는 주로 문장과 문장을 구별하는 음의 높낮이를 의미하는 개념으로서 억양이라고도 합니다. 어떤 문장을 발음하거나 말할 때 음조를 내리면 평서문이 되고 음조를 올리면 의문문이 되는 것은 음조가 문장과 문장을 구별하는 좋은 예입니다.

음조는 평서문과 의문문을 구별하는 기능을 하는 것 외에도 때로는 의문문과 의문문을 구별하는 경우도 있습니다.

1. Jack: John loves Mary, doesn't he? ↑

   Jill: Well, I am not sure, but they seem to be happy together.

2. Bill: John loves Mary, doesn't he? ↓

   Jeanie: Yes, he does.

1번 문장과 2번 문장은 모두 부가의문문(tag question)을 가지고 있는 문장입니다. 부가의문문의 음조를 1번 문장처럼 올리는 경우와 2번 문장처럼 내리는 경우 모두 '존이 메리를 사랑하죠, 그렇지 않나요?'처럼 해석됩니다. 하지만 의미의 차이가 있습니다. 1번 문장처럼 부가의문문의 음조가 올라가는 경우는 말하는 사람인 Jack이 듣는 사람인 Jill이 자신의 의견에 동의할 거라는 확신이 없는 경우입니다. 하지만 2번 문장처럼 부가의문문의 음조가 내려가는 경우는 말하는 사람인 Bill이 듣는 사람인 Jeannie가 자신의 의견에 동의할 거라는 확신이 있는 경우입니다.

이처럼 문장과 문장을 구별하는 음조는 영어에만 있지 않고 한국이, 일본어, 중국어, 스페인어, 러시아어, 등 모든 언어에 다 존재하는 언어 보편적인 현상입니다.

Quiz. "Excuse me"는 "실례합니다" 또는 '실례했습니다"의 의미로 자주 사용됩니다. 그런데 "Excuse me"의 음조가 상향음조(↑)이면 다른 의미를 갖게 됩니다. 상향음조로 발음 되는 "Excuse me"는 어떤 의미일까요?

정답 : 다시 한번 말씀해주세요.

Lecture 2

시제절과 비시제절의 호환성

- 복문에서 수식어인 종속절을 시제절에서 비시제절로 바꾸기

· 주절의 주어와 종속절의 주어가 다른 경우

(1) a. Comp + Subject + Tense + Predicate + Subject + Tense + Neg + Predicate
종속절(시제절) 주절(시제절)

b. Φ + Subject + Φ + (Link) + Predicate + Subject + Tense + Neg + Predicate
종속절(비시제절) 주절(시제절)

- 수식어인 종속절을 시제절에서 비시제절로 바꾸는 과정

· 종속절의 Comp ➡ 생략
· 종속절의 주어 ➡ 생략하지 않음
· 종속절의 동사(Tense, Predicate) ➡ Verb-ing(현재분사)

Ex 1. a. After the work was finished, they went out to relax and have fun.
종속절(시제절) 주절(시제절)

b. The work being finished, they went out to relax and have fun.
종속절(비시제절) 주절(시제절)

Ex 2. a. Though the weather was rainy, they continued the game nevertheless.
종속절(시제절) 주절(시제절)

b. The weather being rainy, they continued the game nevertheless.
종속절(비시제절) 주절(시제절)

Sentence Analysis

(1) a. Though their parent s objected to their marriage, they decided to go through with it nevertheless.

종속절(시제절) / 주절(시제절)

b. Their parents objecting to their marriage, they decided to go through with it nevertheless.

종속절(비시제절) / 주절(시제절)

(2) a. When permission was given, they felt very excited.

종속절(시제절) / 주절(시제절)

b. Permission being given, they felt very excited.

종속절(비시제절) / 주절(시제절)

(3) a. As the day of the wedding approached, the couple began to feel nervous.

종속절(시제절) / 주절(시제절)

b. The day of the wedding approaching, the couple began to feel nervous.

종속절(비시제절) / 주절(시제절)

(4) a. Because coffee was spilled on the wedding dress, Maria almost had a nervous breakdown.

종속절(시제절) / 주절(시제절)

b. Coffee being spilled on the wedding dress, Maria had a nervous breakdown.

종속절(비시제절) / 주절(시제절)

(5) a. When the cake was cut, the audience applauded uproariously.
종속절(시제절) 주절(시제절)

b. The cake being cut, the audience applauded uproariously.
종속절(비시제절) 주절(시제절)

(6) a. Though the day was cloudy, everybody enjoyed the wedding nevertheless.
종속절(시제절) 주절(시제절)

b. The day being cloudy, everybody enjoyed the wedding nevertheless.
종속절(비시제절) 주절(시제절)

(7) a. After the wedding was completely over, the couple felt relieved.
종속절(시제절) 주절(시제절)

b. The wedding being completely over, the couple felt relieved.
종속절(비시제절) 주절(시제절)

(8) a. Because ticket prices rose drastically, they were unable to go on a honeymoon to Hawaii.
종속절(시제절) 주절(시제절)

b. Ticket prices rising drastically, they were unable to go on a honeymoon to Hawaii.
종속절(비시제절) 주절(시제절)

(9) a. When their first child was born, the couple was very happy.
종속절(시제절) 주절(시제절)

b. Their first child being born, they were very happy.
종속절(비시제절) 주절(시제절)

Special Tips on Optionality of Non-progressive "being"

Complex sentences are comprised of main clauses and embedded clauses. The main clauses are almost always tensed clauses; however, the embedded clauses are either tensed clauses or tenseless clauses. There are four types of tenseless clauses: to-infinitive constructions, bare infinitive constructions, gerund constructions, and present participle constructions.

● The Types of Tenseless Embedded Clauses

(1) to-infinitive constructions

Ex

a. John expects (tensed MC) that his son will enter Harvard University. (tensed EC)

b. John expects (tensed MC) his son to enter Harvard University. (tenseless EC)

(2) gerund constructions

Ex

John does not mind (tensed MC) his friends smoking cigarettes in his office. (tensed EC)

(3) bare infinitive construction

Ex

a. Sue saw (tensed MC) that her child opened the door of the refrigerator. (tenseless EC)

b. Sue saw (tensed MC) her child open the door of the refrigerator. (tenseless EC)

(4) present participle constructions

Ex

a. Judy witnessed that her son was smoking a cigar.
tensed MC / tensed EC

b. Judy witnessed her son smoking a cigar.
tensed MC / tenseless EC

c. You should not monopolize the conversation when you talk with your seniors.
tensed MC / tensed EC

d. You should not monopolize the conversation when talking with your seniors.
tensed MC / tenseless EC

- Two Types of "being" in the Present Participle Constructions

(1) obligatory progressive "being"

Ex

Maria heard her son being bullied by his teacher.
tensed MC / tenseless EC

(2) optional non-progressive "being"

Ex

a. The child stopped crying when (being) given something to eat.
tensed MC / tensed EC

b. She began to cry when (being) scolded.
tensed MC / tenseless EC

Dialogue 2

Malcolm : Hey, Wilma. What did your kids get up to today?

Wilma : Well, Malcolm, they had a big exam in the morning. After that, the exam being finished, they went out to play.

Malcolm : After the test was over, they went out to have fun? That reminds me of my old football coach.

Wilma : Your coach? But why? I am dying with curiosity.

Malcolm : Well, we had a huge game at the end of the season, and our coach was always criticizing us. Finally, his team winning the championship, he felt satisfied.

Wilma : After you won the big game, he finally felt satisfied? Actually, that reminds me of my wedding.

Malcolm : Your wedding? How in the world does football remind you of that?

Wilma : Well, I was pretty nervous before the big day. But being married, I felt so relieved.

Malcolm : After you and Bob were married, you felt relieved? Wow, that's some story.

Wilma : Yeah, isn't it great?

Q. 위 대화문에 등장하는 비시제절은 어떤 유형의 구문인가?

① 현재분사 구문 ② to-부정사 구문 ③ 원형부정사 구문 ④ 동명사 구문

정답 : ①

Exercise 1

다음 주어진 예문을 살펴보고 물음에 답하시오.

1. a. You should be careful (주절(시제절)) when you deal with poisonous animals. (종속절(시제절))

   b. You should be careful (주절(시제절)) when dealing with poisonous animals. (종속절(비시제절))

2. a. Since I was employed by the company, (종속절(시제절)) I have worked very hard. (주절(시제절))

   b. Since being employed by the company, (종속절(비시제절)) I have worked very hard. (주절(시제절))

3. a. When night came on, (종속절(시제절)) we started for camp. (주절(시제절))

   b. Night coming on, (종속절(비시제절)) we started for camp. (주절(시제절))

4. a. After the exam was finished, (종속절(시제절)) they went out to relax. (주절(시제절))

   b. The exam being finished, (종속절(비시제절)) they went out to relax. (주절(시제절))

1. 종속절에 complementizer(문장접속사)는 종속절이 시제절에서 비시제절로 바뀌면 사용되는 경우도 있고(1b, 2b) 반드시 생략되어야 하는 경우도(3b, 4b) 있다. 비시제절에서 complementizer가 사용될 수 있는 경우는 사용될 수 없는 경우와 비교해서 어떤 특징이 있나?

____.

Exercise 2

다음 주어진 예문을 살펴보고 물음에 답하시오.

1. a. Judy witnessed (주절(시제절)) that her son was being bullied by a strange man (종속절(시제절)). (1a = 1b)

   b. Judy witnessed (주절(시제절)) her son being bullied by a strange man (종속절(비시제절)).

2. a. Maria heard (주절(시제절)) that her child was being scolded by his teacher (종속절(시제절)). (2a = 2b)

   b. Maria heard (주절(시제절)) her child being scolded by his teacher (종속절(비시제절)).

3. a. The child stopped crying (주절(시제절)) when he was given something to eat (종속절(시제절)). (3a = 3b)

   b. The child stopped crying (주절(시제절)) when being given something to eat (종속절(비시제절)).

4. a. She began to cry (주절(시제절)) when she was scolded (종속절(시제절)). (4a =4b)

   b. She began to cry (주절(시제절)) when being scolded (종속절(비시제절)).

1. 위 보기에 주어진 문장은 모두 a는 시제절이고 b는 비시제절이다. 비시제절에 사용되는 'being'이 진행(progressive aspect)을 나타내는 경우는 어떤 경우인가? (둘을 고르시오)

   ① 1b　　② 2b　　③ 3b　　④ 4b

2. 위 보기에 주어진 문장은 모두 a는 시제절이고 b는 비시제절이다. 비시제절에 사용되는 being이 생략될 수 있는 경우는 어떤 경우인가? (둘을 고르시오)

   ① 1b　　② 2b　　③ 3b　　④ 4b

Exercise 3

1. 주어진 a형 문장의 종속절을 시제절에서 비시제절로 변형시키시오.

① a. When the store opened, the people started shopping.

b. ______________________, the people started shopping.

② a. Though the rain poured, we went on a walk nevertheless.

b. ______________________, we went on a walk nevertheless.

③ a. After the earthquake started, I hid under the bed.

b. ____________________________, I hid under the bed.

④ a. When the curtains closed, the audience applauded uproariously.

b. ________________________, the audience applauded uproariously.

⑤ a. When the rooster crowed, I woke up.

b. ________________________, I woke up.

Wrap Up

시제절과 비시제절의 호환성

● 주절의 주어와 종속절의 주어가 같은 경우

(1) a. Subject + Tense + Neg + Predicate + Comp + Subject + Tense + Predicate
주절(시제절) / 종속절(시제절)

b. Subject + Tense + Neg + Predicate + (Comp) + Φ + Φ + (Link) + Predicate
주절(시제절) / 종속절(비시제절)

- 종속질의 Comp ➡ 필요에 따라서 생략(because, since, as, if)
- 종속절의 주어 ➡ 생략
- 종속절의 동사(Tense, Predicate) ➡ Verb-ing(현재분사)

● 주절의 주어와 종속절의 주어가 다른 경우

(1) a. Comp + Subject + Tense + Predicate + Subject + Tense + Neg + Predicate
종속절(시제절) / 주절(시제절)

b. Φ + Subject + Φ + (Link) + Predicate + Subject + Tense + Neg + Predicate
종속절(비시제절) / 주절(시제절)

- 종속절의 Comp ➡ 생략
- 종속절의 주어 ➡ 생략하지 않음
- 종속절의 동사(Tense, Predicate) ➡ Verb-ing(현재분사)

UNIT 10

수동구문에 대한 이해

What is a passivization?

Warm Up

문장을 구성하는 기본 문장 성분은 Comp, Subject, Tense, Neg, Link, Aspect, Predicate 입니다. 이러한 7가지 기본 문장성분을 이용해서 능동구문과 수동구문의 유기적인 상관관계를 원리적으로 설명할 수 있습니다.

1. Passivization

- 능동구문과 수동구문의 문장구조

a. Subject + (Tense) + (Link) + (Aspect) + Predicate-2 + Obj
b. Subject + (Tense) + (Link) + (Aspect) + Passive Predicate-1 + by + NP

- 능동구문에서 수동구문으로의 변화과정

a. 술어역할을 하는 타동사 ➔ 수동형 과거분사
b. 술어역할을 하는 타동사가 수동형 과거분사로 바뀌면서 사라진 정보를 Tense, Link, 또는 Aspect 자리에 보충

- 술어의 사라진 정보를 보충하는 과정

a. 시제가 사라진 경우 ➡ Tense 자리에 시제를 보충

b. 진행(progressive aspect)의 의미가 사라진 경우 ➡ Aspect 자리에 "being"을 추가

c. 완료(perfect aspect)의 의미가 사라진 경우 ➡ Aspect 자리에 "been"을 추가

d. 술어가 동사원형에서 수동형 과거분사로 바뀐 경우 ➡ Link 자리에 "be"를 추가

e. 술어가 동명사에서 수동형 과거분사로 바뀐 경우 ➡ Link 자리에 "being"을 추가

Quiz on Today's Lessons

1. a. John pushed the button.
   b. The button was pushed by John.

2. a. Sue was talking to a strange man.
   b. A strange man was being talked to by Sue.

3. a. Jack has invited two friends.
   b. Two friends have been invited by Jack.

4. a. Brian will employ two men.
   b. Two men will be employed by Brian.

1. 문장 (1a)의 transitive predicate "pushed"가 문장 (1b)의 passive predicate "pushed"로 변화되면서 상실된 정보는 무엇인가?

① 현재시제(present tense) ② 과거시제(past tense)

③ 진행상(progressive aspect) ④ 완료상(perfect aspect)

2. 상실된 정보를 back up하기 위해서 문장 (1b)에서 새롭게 추가된 단어는 무엇인가?

① the button ② was ③ by ④ John

3. 문장 (2a)의 transitive predicate "talking to"가 문장 (1b)의 passive predicate "talked to"로 변화되면서 상실된 정보는 무엇인가?

① 현재시제(present tense) ② 과거시제(past tense)
③ 진행상(progressive aspect) ④ 완료상(perfect aspect)

4. 상실된 정보를 back up하기 위해서 문장 (2b)에서 새롭게 추가된 단어는 무엇인가?

① being ② was ③ by ④ a strange man

5. 문장 (3a)의 perfective transitive predicate "invited"가 문장 (1b)의 passive predicate "invited"로 변화되면서 상실된 정보는 무엇인가?

① 현재시제(present tense) ② 과거시제(past tense)
③ 진행상(progressive aspect) ④ 완료상(perfective aspect)

6. 문장 (4a)의 bare infinitive transitive predicate "employ"가 문장 (4b)의 passive predicate "employed"로 변화되면서 새롭게 추가된 동사 "be"의 문장성분은 무엇인가?

① 보문어(complementizer) ② 시제(tense) ③ 상(aspect) ④ 연결어(link)

Lecture 1

능동구문과 수동구문의 호환성

- Model of Passivization

a. Subj + (Tense) + (Neg) + (Link) + (Aspect) + Predicate-2 + Obj

b. Subj + (Tense) + (Neg) + (Link) + (Aspect) + Passive Predicate-1 + by + NP

- Process of Passivization

a. 술어역할을 하는 타동사 ➡ 수동형 과거분사

b. 술어가 타동사에서 수동형 과거분사로 바뀌면서 사라진 정보를 Tense, Link, 또는 Aspect에 보충

- **술어의 사라진 정보를 보충하는 과정**

a. 시제가 사라진 경우 ➡ Tense 자리에 시제를 보충

b. 진행(progressive aspect)의 의미가 사라진 경우 ➡ Aspect 자리에 "being"을 추가

c. 완료(perfective aspect)의 의미가 사라진 경우 ➡ Aspect 자리에 "been"을 추가

d. 술어가 동사원형에서 수동형 과거분사로 바뀐 경우 ➡ Link 자리에 "be"를 추가

e. 술어가 동명사에서 수동형 과거분사로 바뀐 경우 ➡ Link 자리에 "being"을 추가

- Examples of Passivization

a. lost information of tense backed up in Tense

Subject + (Tense) + (Neg) + (Link) + (Aspect) + Predicate-2 + Object

Ex 1

a. Servicemen	fix	computers.
Subj	Pred-2	Obj

b. Computers	are	fixed	by servicemen.
Subj	Tense	Pred-1	Mod

Ex 2

a. An automechanic	repaired	her car.
Subj	Pred-2	Obj

b. Her car	was	repaired	by an automechanic.
Subj	Tense	Pred-1	Mod

b. linking verb "be" backed up in Link

Subject + (Tense) + (Neg) + (Link) + (Aspect) + Predicate-2 + Object

Ex 1

a. Mr. Park	will	not	teach	English phonics.
Subj	Tense	Neg	Pred-2	Obj

b. English phonics	will	not	be	taught	by Mr. Park.
Subj	Tense	Neg	Link	Pred-1	Mod

Ex 2

a. The CEO	will	not	scold	the new secretary.
Subj	Tense	Neg	Pred-2	Obj

b. The new secretary	will	not	be	scolded	by the CEO.
Subj	Tense	Neg	Link	Pred-1	Mod

c. progressive verb "being" backed up in Aspect

Subject + (Tense) + (Neg) + (Link) + (Aspect) + Predicate-2 + Object

Ex1

a. Mrs. Kim	will	be		cleaning	the living room	between 3 and 5 pm.	
Subj	Tense	Link		Pred-2	Obj	Mod	
b. The living room	will	be	being	cleaned	by Mrs. Kim	between 3 and 5 pm.	
Subj	Tense	Link	Asp	Pred-1	Mod	Mod	

Ex2

a. A pop singer	will	be		singing	new songs	for a long time.
Subj	Tense	Link		Pred-2	Obj	Mod
b. New songs	will	be	being	sung	by a pop singer	for a long time.
Subj	Tense	Link	Asp	Pred-1	Mod	Mod

d. perfective verb "been" backed up in Aspect

Subject + (Tense) + (Neg) + (Link) + (Aspect) + Predicate-2 + Object

Ex

a. He	will	not	have		completed	the project	by then.
Subj	Tense	Neg	Link		Pred-2	Obj	Mod
b. The project	will	not	have	been	completed	by him	by then.
Subj	Tense	Neg	Link	Aspect	Pred-1	Mod	Mod

Special Tips on Purpose of Passivization

- The Purpose of Passivization

a. Emphasizing the subject by placing it at sentence-final position

Ex1 a. Columbus discovered new land.
b. New land was discovered by Columbus.

Ex2 a. Booth assassinated Lincoln.
b. Lincoln was assassinated by Booth.

b. Elimination of noninformative subject

Ex1 a. They constructed a new bridge last year.
b. A new bridge was constructed last year.

Ex2 a. Sombody cleans the room every day.
b. The room is cleaned every day.

Dialogue 1

Tony : Oh, no! Our dog Poofy ate our dinner.

Jane : Surely you jest. It cannot be that our dinner was eaten by our dog Poofy! He is far too sweet a dog.

Tony : Sweet? I don't think so. He's completely worthless. Poofy will not even do any tricks.

Jane : It's true that tricks will not be done by Poofy, but that's because he is too classy. He doesn't want to.

Tony : You're crazy. That dog of yours needs some mental help. Both of you should go to doggy school.

Jane : I will not be attending doggy school!

Poofy : Ruff! Ruff!

Jane : You tell him, Poofy!

Q. 위 대화문에서 "Ruff! Ruff!"는 무슨 의미인가?

① I will be attending doggy school.

② I will not be attending doggy school, either.

정답 : ②

Exercise 1

1. 다음 밑줄 친 주어진 문장을 수동태 구문으로 변형하시오. 단 능동구문의 주어를 생략하시오.

(1) a. Somebody stole a lot of money in the robbery.

b. A lot of money ______________________.

(2) a. Somebody has cleaned the office.

b. The office ______________________.

(3) a. Somebody is using the computer at the moment.

b. The computer ______________________ at the moment.

2. Complete the sentences with the verbs in the box.

(1) a. John praised Sue for her success.

b. Sue (   ) praised for her success by John.

(2) a. Mr. Kim takes care of two dogs.

b. Two dogs (   ) taken care of by Mr. Kim.

(3) a. Susan is talking to a strange man.

b. A strange man is (   ) talked to by Susan.

(4) a. The boss has employed two young men.

b. Two young men have (   ) employed by the boss.

(5) a. Jina will kiss him tonight.

b. He will (   ) kissed by Jina tonight.

3. 다음 쌍으로 된 문장들은 의미가 동일 한 문장이다. 밑줄 친 단어들은 문장에서 무슨 역할을 하는가? 보기에서 고르시오.

Ex 진행상, 완료상, 연결어, 시제

(1) a. Children are bothering their parents.

b. Parents are being bothered by their children.

(2) a. I do not like people telling me what to do.

b. I do not like being told what to do.

(3) a. She hates people keeping her waiting.

b. She hates being kept waiting.

(4) a. Though she is pretty, she is not popular with boys.

b. Though being pretty, she is not popular with boys.

4. 다음은 단문의 수동태과정에 대한 설명이다. 빈 칸에 들어갈 적절한 단어를 채워 넣으시오.

a. Subj + (Tense) + (Neg) + (Link) + (Aspect) + Predicate-2 + Object
b. Subj + (Tense) + (Neg) + (Link) + (Aspect) + Passive Predicate-1 + by + NP

(1) 술어 자리의 동사가 시제동사인 경우는 술어동사를 수동형 과거분사로 변형시킨 후 상실된 시제 정보를 보충하기 위해서 (   ) 동사를 시제자리에 채워 넣는다.

① be (am, are, is, was, were) ② have (have, has, had)
③ do (do, does, did) ④ may

(2) 술어 자리에 있는 동사가 진행형 동사인 경우는 술어동사를 수동형 과거분사로 변형시킨 후 상실된 진행 정보를 보충하기 위해서 (   )을/를 Aspect 자리에 넣는다.

① being ② been ③ be ④ having

(3) 술어 자리에 있는 동사가 완료형 동사인 경우는 술어동사를 수동형 과거분사로 변형시킨 후 상실된 완료를 보충하기 위해서 (   )을/를 Aspect 자리에 넣는다.

① being ② been ③ be ④ having

(4) 술어 자리에 있는 동사가 동사원형인 경우는 술어동사를 수동형 과거분사로 변형시킨 후 (   )을/를 Link 자리에 넣는다.

① being ② been ③ be ④ having

바벨탑과 언어의 분화

구약성경에 보면 인간이 바벨탑(Tower of Babel)을 만들어 하늘 높이 오르려고 시도했던 사건이 나온다. 바벨탑을 만들어 하늘 높이 오르려했던 인간의 시도가 창조주의 뜻에 합당하지 않았고, 그 결과 언어가 혼잡해지면서 서로 다른 언어가 사용되기 시작했다. 만약 인간이 바벨탑을 만들지 않았더라면 인류는 오늘날 하나의 언어를 사용하고 있을지도 모른다.

바벨탑 사건 이후로 인간은 서로 다른 언어를 사용하기 시작했고 오늘날 지구상에는 약 200여 개의 언어가 존재한다. 지구상에 존재하는 이러한 언어들은 서로 다른 양상을 보이지만 성서의 관점에서 보자면 원래는 하나의 언어였기 때문에 비슷한 점도 있다.

서로 다른 언어들이 보이는 공통점 중에 하나는 부정에서 찾아 볼 수 있다. 대부분의 언어에서 부정을 나타내는 말에는 비음(nasal sound)이 들어간다. 영어의 'no,' 불어의 'non,' 독어의 'nein,' 이탈리아어의 'no,' 러시아어의 'niet,' 스페인어의 'no,' 한국어의 'an,' 그리고 일본어의 'nai'와 같은 부정을 나타내는 말을 보면 모두 비음 즉 콧소리가 들어간다. 이러한 공통점은 우연이라기보다도 언어가 원래 하나의 기원에서 나왔기 때문에 생기는 필연적 결과일 가능성이 높다.

Quiz. 'non'은 불어에서 사용되는 부정어, 'nein'은 독일어에서 사용되는 부정어, 그리고 'niet'는 러시아어에서 사용되는 부정어다. 그렇다면 'khong' 어느 언어에서 사용되는 부정어인가?

① 폴란드어 ② 히브리어 ③ 그리스어 ④ 베트남어

정답 : ④

Lecture 2

비시제절 종속절의 수동태

- Model of Passivization

a. Subj + (Tense) + (Neg) + (Link) + (Aspect) + Predicate +

주절(시제절)

Subj + (Tense) + (Neg) + (Link) + (Aspect) + Predicate-2 + Obj

종속절(비시제절)

b. Subj + (Tense) + (Neg) + (Link) + (Aspect) + Predicate +

주절(시제절)

(Subj) + (Tense) + (Neg) + (Link) + (Aspect) + Passive Pred-1+ by + NP

종속절(비시제절)

- 비시제절 종속절의 수동태 과정

a. 술어 역할을 하는 타동사 ➡ 수동형 과거분사

b. 술어 역할을 하는 타동사가 수동형 과거분사로 바뀌면서 사라진 정보를 Link, 또는 Aspect에 보충

- 술어의 사라진 정보를 보충하는 과정

a. 술어가 동명사에서 수동형 과거분사로 바뀐 경우 ➡ Link 자리에 "being"을 추가

b. 술어가 동사원형에서 수동형 과거분사로 바뀐 경우 ➡ Link 자리에 "be"를 추가

c. 술어가 완료형에서 수동형 과거분사로 바뀐 경우 ➡ Aspect 자리에 "been"을 추가

● Examples of Passivization of Tenseless Embedded Clauses

· linking verb "being" backed up in Link

(1) a.	He	does	not	like	strange people	talking to	his wife.
	Subj	Tense	Neg	Pred	Subj	Pred-2	Obj

b.	He	does	not	like	his wife	being	talked to	by strange people.
	Subj	Tense	Neg	Pred	Subj	Link	Pred-1	Mod

(2) a.	She	hates	ladies	visiting	her husband	too often.
	Subj	Pred	Sub	Pred-2	Obj	Mod

b.	She	hates	her husband	being	visited	by ladies	too often.
	Subj	Pred	Subj	Link	Pred-1	Mod	Mod

(3) a.	She	dislikes	the homeroom teacher	bullying	her son.
	Subj	Pred	Subj	Pred-2	Mod

b.	She	dislikes	her son	being	bullied	by the homeroom teacher.
	Subj	Pred	Sub	Link	Pred-1	Mod

(4) a.	Jimmy	doesn't	like	people	telling	him	what to do.
	Subj	Tense	Pred	Sub	Pred-3	IO	DO

b.	Jimmy	does	not	like	being	told	what to do.
	Subj	Tense	Neg	Pred	Link	Pred-2	Obj

(5) a.	Sue	hates	her parents	treating	her	like a child.
	Subj	Pred	Sub	Pred-3	Obj	Manner

b.	Sue	hates	being	treated	like a child	by her parents.
	Subj	Pred	Link	Pred-2	Manner	Mod

(6) a.

Mr. Kim	does	not	mind	his students	asking	him	difficult questions.
Subj	Tense	Neg	Pred	Subj	Pred-3	IO	DO

b.

Mr. Kim	does	not	mind	being	asked	difficult questions	by his students.
Subj	Tense	Neg	Pred	Link	Pred-2	Obj	Mod

· linking verb "be" backed up in Link

(1) a.

When studying,	Jenny	does	not	want	her family	to	talk to	her.
Mod	Subj	Tense	Neg	Pred	Sub	Link	Pred-2	Obj

b.

When studying,	Jenny	does	not	want	to be	talked to	by her family.
Mod	Subj	Tense	Neg	Pred	Link	Pred-1	Mod

(2) a.

Maria	expects	people	to	treat	her	like a princess.
Subj	Pred	Sub	Link	Pred-3	Obj	Manner

b.

Maria	expects	to be	treated	like a princess	by people.
Subj	Pred	Link	Pred-2	Manner	Mod

· aspectual verb "been" backed up in Aspect

(1) a.

Sue	remembers	her brother	having	bullied	her pet.
Subj	Pred	Subj	Link	Pred-2	Obj

b.

Sue	remembers	her pet	having	been	bullied	by her brother.
Subj	Pred	Subj	Link	Asp	Pred-1	Mod

(2) a.

He	appreciates	his parents	having	taken care of	his son	during his absence.
Subj	Pred	Subj	Link	Pred-2	Obj	Mod

b.

He	appreciates	his son	having	been	taken care of	by his parents	during his absence.
Subj	Pred	Subj	Link	Asp	Pred-1	Mod	Mod

(3) a.

She	will	not	forget	her husband	having	shouted at	her.
Subj	Tense	Neg	Pred	Subj	Link	Pred-2	Obj

b.

She	will	not	forget	having	been	shouted at	by her husband.
Subj	Tense	Neg	Pred	Link	Asp	Pred-1	Mod

(4) a.

Bill	does	not	resent	his old friend	having	taken advantage of	him.
Subj	Tense	Neg	Pred	Subj	Link	Pred-2	Mod

b.

Bill	does	not	resent	having	been	taken advantage of	by his old friend.
Subj	Tense	Neg	Pred	Link	Asp	Pred-1	Mod

Special Tips on the Subject of Tenseless Clauses

1. Subject of Tensed Embedded Clauses

(1) a. John does not believe (tensed main clause) that his son has bullied him. (tensed embedded clause)

b. John does not think (tensed main clause) that he has been bullied by his son. (tensed embedded clause)

(2) a. Sue does not think (tensed main clause) that he has deceived her. (tensed embedded clause)

b. She does not think (tensed main clause) that she has been deceived by him. (tensed embedded clause)

- Tensed embedded clauses almost always have a subject, regardless of whether they the subject of the embedded clause and the subject of the main clause refer to the same person or not.

2. Subject of Tenseless Embedded Clauses

(1) a. He does not like (tensed main clause) strange people talking to his wife. (tenseless embedded clause)

b. He does not like (tensed main clause) his wife being talked to by strange people. (tenseless embedded clause)

(2) a. Bill does not resent his old friend having taken advantage of him.

tensed main clause — tenseless embedded clause

b. Bill does not resent having been taken advantage of by his old friend.

tensed main clause — tenseless embedded clause

- Tenseless embedded clauses have a subject only when the person that the subject of the embedded clause refers to is different from the person that the subject of the main clause refers to. If the person that subject of the embedded clause refers to is the same person that the subject of the main clause refers to, then the subject of the embedded clause is omitted.

Dialogue 2

Sue : John really is bossy!

Tom : What do you mean?

Sue : I do not like people telling me what to do.

Tom : No one does. What's your point?

Sue : I'm saying John is always giving orders, not requests. I do not like being told what to do.

Tom : Oh, I see what you mean. He's also not very patient. I feel sorry for his wife, Mary.

Sue : Right! John hates Mary keeping him waiting. But, he is sometimes late himself!

Tom : Well, I know John hates being kept waiting by Mary, but you have to admit Mary is ALWAYS late, and that can be annoying.

Sue : That's true.

Tom : So why are we talking about John anyway?

Sue : Oh, because we both forgot our office keys, so John insisted I climb over the front wall with him.

Tom : What? That's crazy! The security guard has a big dog you know!

Sue : I know. We managed to climb the wall without anybody seeing us. It was a little scary.

Tom : I can't believe you did that in that skirt and high heels! What if someone had seen you? It could have been really embarrassing.

Sue : We managed to climb the wall without being seen. So I think I'm ok.

Tom : What about the security camera?

Sue : The what?!

Q. 위 대화문에서 붉은색으로 표시된 'being'의 역할은 무엇인가?

① Tense ② Link ③ Aspect ④ Predicate

정답 : ②

Exercise 1

1. 다음은 비시제절인 종속절의 수동태과정에 대한 설명이다. 빈 칸에 들어갈 적절한 단어를 채워 넣으시오.

비시제절인 종속절의 수동태

a. Subj + (Tense) + (Neg) + (Link) + (Aspect) + Predicate
주절(시제절)

+ Subj + (Tense) + (Neg) + (Link) + (Aspect) + Predicate + Obj
종속절(비시제절)

b. Subj + (Tense) + (Neg) + (Link) + (Aspect) + Predicate
주절(시제절)

+ (Subj) + (Tense) + (Neg) + (Link) + (Aspect) + Passive Predicate + by + NP
종속절(비시제절)

(1) 종속절의 술어 자리에 있는 동사가 동명사(gerund)인 경우는 술어동사를 수동형 과거분사로 변형시킨 후 주절 술어와 종속절 술어의 연결을 위해 being을 (   ) 자리에 넣는다.

① Tense   ② Neg   ③ Link   ④ Aspect

(2) 종속절의 술어 자리에 있는 동사가 완료형 동사인 경우는 술어동사를 수동형 과거분사로 변형시킨 후 상실된 완료를 보충하기 위해서 been을 (   ) 자리에 넣는다.

① Tense   ② Neg   ③ Link   ④ Aspect

(3) 종속절이 비시제절인 경우 종속절의 주어가 주절의 주어와 (   ) 사람이면 생략하고 (   ) 사람이면 생략하지 않는다.

① 동일한, 다른   ② 다른, 동일한

2. 다음 주어진 문장의 종속절을 수동구문으로 변형시키시오.

(1) a. Bill does not like people touching his baby.

b. Bill does not like his baby (   ) (   ) by people.

(2) a. Mary dislikes her parents treating her like a child.

b. Mary dislikes (   ) (   ) like a child by her parents.

(3) a. He does not expect his parents to treat him like a prince.

b. He does not expect (   ) (   ) treated like a prince by his parents.

(4) a. Mary resents her husband having forgotten her birthday.

b. Mary resents her birthday having (   ) (   ) by her husband.

(5) a. Jina does not mind her children having bothered her for a long time.

b. Jina does not mind (   ) (   ) bothered by her children for a long time.

Wrap Up

Model of Passivization Process

a. Sub + (Tense) + (Neg) + (Link) + (Aspect) + Predicate-2 + Obj

b. Subj + (Tense) + (Neg) + (Link) + (Aspect) + Passive Predicate-1 + by + NP

Process of Passivization

- **transitive predicate with tense**

  a. transitive predicate with tense ➡ passive predicate

  b. lost tense information is backed up in Tense

- **transitive predicate with progressive aspect**

  a. transitive predicate with progressive aspect ➡ passive predicate

  b. progressive verb “being” is backed up in Aspect

- **transitive predicate with perfective aspect**

  a. transitive predicate with perfective aspect ➡ passive predicate

  b. perfective verb “been” is backed up in Aspect

- **transitive infinitive predicate**

  a. transitive infinitive ➡ passive predicate

  b. linking verb “be” is backed up in Link

- **transitive gerund predicate**

  a. transitive infinitive ➡ passive predicate

  b. linking verb “being” backed up in Link

Memo

UNIT 11 종속절의 주어는 어디로 갔을까?

Where is the embedded clause subject?

Warm Up

문장을 구성하는 기본 문장 성분은 Comp, Subject, Tense, Neg, Link, Aspect, Predicate 입니다. Predicate이 1가 술어인 경우 하나의 문장성분이 필요하며, 2가 술어인 경우 2개의 문장성분이 필요합니다. 3가 술어의 경우는 세 개의 문장성분이 필요합니다.

1. Types of Predicates

- 1-Place Predicate → one sentence element
- 2-Place Predicate → two sentence elements
- 3-Place Predicate → three sentence elements

하나의 문장성분을 필요로 하는 1가 술어는 주어를 필요로 하는 1가 술어와 명제를 필요로 하는 1가 술어로 구분할 수 있습니다.

2. One-Place Predicates with Subjects

- a. Comp + Subj + Tense + Neg + Predicate-1
  b. Comp + Expletive + Tense + Neg + Subj

a. That John will pass the exam is possible.

b. It is possible that John will pass the exam.

1가 술어가 취하는 주어는 원칙적으로 술어 앞에 위치하지만 주어가 절(clause)인 경우는 균형을 위해 문장 끝에 위치할 수도 있습니다.

3. One-Place Predicates with Propositions

- a. Comp + Expletive + Tense + Neg + Predicate-1 + Proposition

  b. Comp + Subj + Tense + Neg + Predicate-1 + Proposition

a. It is likely that John will pass the exam.

b. John is likely to pass the exam.

1가 술어가 취하는 명제는 절(clause)로 되어 있으며 언제나 술어 뒤에 위치합니다. 명제와 주어의 가장 큰 차이점은 명제의 경우는 종속절의 주어가 주절의 주어 자리로 이동할 수 있다는 점입니다.

Quiz on Today's Lessons

Ex

1\. a. It (Ex) is (Tense) impossible (Pred-1) that John will break up with his girlfriend. (Subj)

b. John (Subj) is (Tense) impossible (Pred-1) to break up with his girlfriend. (Subj) (= 비문)

2\. a. It (Ex) is (Tense) unlikely (Pred-1) that John will break up with his girlfriend. (Proposition)

b. John (Subj) is (Tense) unlikely (Pred-1) to break up with his girlfriend. (Proposition)

위 보기에 주어진 예문을 보면 종속절의 주어가 주절의 주어자리로 이동할 수 있는 경우도 있고 이동할 수 없는 경우도 있다. 종속절의 주어가 주절의 주어자리로 이동할 수 있는지 여부는 주절의 술어가 보기 1a의 **impossible**처럼 주어를 취하는 1가 술어인지 아니면 1b의 **unlikely**처럼 명제(proposition)를 취하는 1가 술어인지에 달려있다. 다음에 주어진 1가 술어가 명제를 취하는 1가 술어인지 주어를 취하는 1가 술어인지 명시하시오.

A형. Comp + Expletive + Tense + Predicate-1 + Subject

B형. Comp + Expletive + Tense + Predicate-1 + Proposition

(1) seem A형 B형

(2) easy A형 B형

(3) prove A형 B형

(4) possible A형 B형

(5) turn out A형 B형

(6) difficult A형 B형

(7) probable A형 B형

(8) certain A형 B형

(9) appear A형 B형

(10) likely A형 B형

Lecture 1

종속절 주어 ➡ 주절의 주어

● One-place Predicate **Sentences with Propositions**

(1) a. Comp + Expl + Tense + Neg + Link + Aspect + Predicate-1 +
주절

Comp + Subj + Tense + Neg + Link + Aspect + Predicate
종속절(명제)

b. Comp + Subj + Tense + Neg + Link + Aspect + Predicate-1 +
주절

(　　　) + (　　　) + (　　　) + Neg + Link + Aspect + Predicate
종속절(명제)

Sentence Analysis

(1) a. It seems (주절) that golf is one of the most popular of all outdoor sports. (종속절)

b. Golf seems (주절) to be one of the most popular of all outdoor sports. (종속절)

(2) a. It appears (주절) that more than one million people are enjoying golf in the world. (종속절)

b. More than one million people appear (주절) to be enjoying golf in the world. (종속절)

(3) a. It is said that the standard golf course consists of eighteen holes.

주절 종속절

b. The standard golf course is said to consist of eighteen holes.

주절 종속절

(4) a. It is well known that golfers wear leather gloves to ensure a firm grip.

주절 종속절

b. Golfers are well known to wear leather gloves to ensure a firm grip.

주절 종속절

(5) a. It is not likely for golfers to carry more than fourteen clubs in their bags.

주절 종속절

b. Golfers are not likely to carry more than fourteen clubs in their bags.

주절 종속절

(6) a. It is known that golf balls used in the States are a little bigger than British balls.

주절 종속절

b. Golf balls used in the States are known to be a little bigger than British balls.

주절 종속절

(7) a. It is reported that rich golfers spend more than one million dollars on equipment.

주절 종속절

b. Rich golfers are reported to spend more than one million dollars on equipment.

주절 종속절

(8) a. It is said / that par is the score that an expert golfer would make on a given hole.
주절 / 종속절

b. Par is said / to be the score that an expert golfer would make on a given hole.
주절 / 종속절

(9) a. It is expected / that professional golfers should get a birdie very often.
주절 / 종속절

b. Professional golfers are expected / to get a birdie very often.
주절 / 종속절

(10) a. It is generally assumed / that an eagle is worth the same as a hole-in-one.
주절 / 종속절

b. An eagle is generally assumed / to be worth the same as a hole-in-one.
주절 / 종속절

Special Tips on Subject-to-Subject Raising

The Purpose of Subject-to-Subject Raising

1. a. It seems that John is late for the meeting.
   b. John seems to be late for the meeting.

In sentence (1a), the verb *seems* is a one-place predicate. It selects the embedded clause that *John is late for the meeting* as a proposition. In sentence (1b), the subject of the embedded clause, *John*, undergoes movement to the main clause subject position. Sentences (1a) and (1b) are semantically interchangeable, but they are slightly different in meaning. Sentence (1a) expresses a stronger assertion that John will be late for the meeting than sentence (1b). For example, sentence (1a) expresses a more judgemental mood of the speaker that John will be late for the meeting. On the other hand, sentence (1b) expresses a less judgemental mood of the speaker that John will be late for the meeting. Diminution of the speaker's assertion is not only true for sentences with *seem*, but also for sentences with other one-place predicates with propositions.

2. a. It is likely that Sue will win a scholarship.
   b. Sue is likely to win a scholarship.
3. a. It appears that Sue is smarter than her sister.
   b. Sue appears to be smarter than her sister.
4. a. It is unlikely that Jina will get admission to the university.
   b. Jina is unlikely to get admission to the university.

Therefore we can say that the subject-to-subject raising diminishes the judgemental aspect of the proposition.

Dialogue 1

Harry : There is likely to be a storm soon.

Sue : I know that it is likely that there will be a storm soon. You're not the only one who watches the weather channel, dear.

Harry : My, my! Well, I bet there is something I know that you don't.

Sue : I highly doubt it, but let me hear it.

Harry : Oh ye of little faith! This news is certain to shock you.

Sue : Spit it out! Don't keep me waiting.

Harry : Well, you know Jack and Jill who live just up the hill from us?

Sue : Of course. Jill and I are in constant competition for making the best pie.

Harry : Well, the perfect couple is getting a divorce.

Sue : Oh, my! Jack and Jill were so unlikely to break up.

Harry : You speak the truth, woman. It was indeed unlikely that Jack and Jill would break up, but alas, the unthinkable has occurred.

Sue : What will happen next?

Harry : One can never know…

Q. 위 대화문에서 종속절의 주어가 주절의 주어로 이동하는 예를 보이는 술어는 무엇인가? (둘을 고르시오)

① likely ② unlikely ③ certain ④ occur

정답 : ①, ②

Exercise 1

1. a. It is not easy for mediocre men to win women's hearts. (O)

   주절 (It is not easy) / 종속절 (for mediocre men to win women's hearts)

   b. Mediocre men are not easy to win women's hearts. (×)

   주절 (Mediocre men are not easy) / 종속절 (to win women's hearts)

2. a. It is possible for attractive women to win men's hearts. (O)

   주절 (It is possible) / 종속절 (for attractive women to win men's hearts)

   b. Attractive women are possible to win men's hearts. (×)

   주절 (Attractive women are possible) / 종속절 (to win men's hearts)

3. a. It is probable that appearance has a genetic element. (O)

   주절 (It is probable) / 종속절 (that appearance has a genetic element)

   b. Appearance is probable to have a genetic element. (×)

   주절 (Appearance is probable) / 종속절 (to have a genetic element)

1. 위 보기에 주어진 술어의 공통점은 무엇인가?

① 명제를 취하는 1가 술어　② 주어를 취하는 1가 술어

③ 주어와 목적어를 취하는 2가 술어　④ 주어와 주격보어를 취하는 2가 술어

2. 위 보기에 주어진 문장에서 a형 문장이 b형 문장으로 바뀌기 위해서 일어난 변형은 무엇인가?

① 종속절 주어의 이동　② 종속절 목적어의 이동

③ 주절 주어의 이동　④ 주절 목적어의 이동

1. a. It is unlikely (주절) for mediocre men to win women's hearts (종속절). (O)

b. Mediocre men are unlikely (주절) to win women's hearts (종속절). (O)

2. a. It is certain (주절) that attractive women will win men's hearts (종속절). (O)

b. Attractive women are certain (주절) to win men's hearts (종속절). (O)

3. a. It seems (주절) that appearance has a genetic element (종속절). (O)

b. Appearance seems (주절) to have a genetic element (종속절). (O)

3. 위 보기에 주어진 술어의 공통점은 무엇인가?

① 명제를 취하는 1가 술어
② 주어를 취하는 1가 술어
③ 주어와 목적어를 취하는 2가 술어
④ 주어와 주격보어를 취하는 2가 술어

4. 위 보기에 주어진 문장에서 a형 문장과 b형 문장의 의미적인 차이점은 무엇인가?

① a형 문장이 b형 문장보다 더 강한 선언적 의미를 가지고 있다.
② b형 문장이 a형 문장보다 더 강한 선언적 의미를 가지고 있다.
③ a형 문장이 b형 문장보다 더 부드러운 표현방법이다.
④ 두 문장이 의미의 차이가 전혀 없다.

1. a. It is said that the standard golf course consists of either nine or eighteen holes.
   주절 / 종속절

   b. The standard golf course is said **to** consist of either nine or eighteen holes.
   주절 / 종속절

2. a. It is said that the golf balls used in the States are a little bigger than British balls.
   주절 / 종속절

   b. The golf balls used in the States are said **to be** a little bigger than British balls.
   주절 / 종속절

5. 위 보기에 1a의 종속절의 주어가 주절 주어로 이동하면 1b의 문장이 형성된다. 문장 1b의 종속절에서 to의 역할은 무엇인가?

① Tense ② Link ③ Comp ④ Aspect

6. 위 보기에 2a의 종속절의 주어가 주절 주어로 이동하면 2b의 문장이 형성된다. 문장 2b의 종속절에서 to be의 역할은 무엇인가?

① Tense ② Link ③ Comp ④ Aspect

1. a. It seems that John **is** a rich man.
주절 종속절

b. John seems **to be** a rich man.
주절 종속절

2. a. It seems that John **has** been a rich man.
주절 종속절

b. John seems **to have** been a rich man.
주절 종속절

3. a. It seemed that John **was** a rich man.
주절 종속절

b. John seemed **to be** a rich man.
주절 종속절

4. a. It seemed that John **had** been a rich man.
주절 종속절

b. John seemed **to have** been a rich man.
주절 종속절

5. a. It seems that John **was** a rich man.
주절 종속절

b. John seems **to have** been a rich man.
주절 종속절

7. 위 보기의 문장들은 종속절의 주어가 주절의 주어자리로 이동하는 과정을 보여주고 있다. 종속절의 주어가 주절의 주어로 이동하면 종속절의 시제동사는 "to + 동사원형"의 형태로 바뀐다. 그런데 종속절의 시제동사가 "to + 동사원형"의 형태로 바뀌지 않고 "to + have + 완료형분사"의 형태로 바뀌는 경우는 어떤 경우인가?

① 주절과 종속절이 모두 현재인 경우

② 주절과 종속절이 모두 과거인 경우

③ 주절은 현재이고 종속절은 과거인 경우

④ 주절은 과거이고 종속절은 현재인 경우

Coffee Break

Euphemism in American Culture

Overweight Auditor: It seems that there are some tax cheats in your company.

Euphemistic President: No, we are just mathematically challenged.

Overweight Auditor: Hmm, then I don't understand people calling me Mr. Overweight. I'm just horizontally challenged.

미국문화와 완곡어법

뚱뚱한 회계감사원: 당신 회사에서 탈세를 좀 하신 것 같습니다.

완곡어법을 좋아하는 사장님: 아니지요. 우린 단지 산술적으로 조금 잘 못 되었을 뿐입니다.

뚱뚱한 회계감사원: 음, 그렇다면 나를 뚱보라고 부르는 사람을 이해하지 못하겠소. 난 단지 수평적으로 조금 잘 못 되었을 뿐이라오.

Quiz. 완곡어법의 하나인 'vertically challenged'는 무슨 의미인가?

① 뚱뚱한 사람　　② 키가 작은 사람

정답 : ②

Lecture 2

종속절 주어 ➡ 주절의 주어

- One-place Predicate Sentences with Propositions

(1) a. Comp + Expl + Tense + Neg + Link + Aspect + Predicate-1 +
주절

Comp + Sub + Tense + Neg + Link + Aspect + Predicate
종속절(명제)

b. Comp + Subj + Tense + Neg + Link + Aspect + Predicate-1 +
주절

(   ) + (   ) + (   ) + Neg + Link + Aspect + Predicate
종속절(명제)

Sentence Analysis

(1) a. It seems (주절) that Jennifer has an exceptional talent for golf. (종속절)

b. Jennifer seems (주절) to have an exceptional talent for golf. (종속절)

(2) a. It is believed (주절) that she is the best golfer from her town. (종속절)

b. She is believed (주절) to be the best golfer from her town. (종속절)

(3) a. It appears (주절) that she is loved by her fans. (종속절)

b. She appears (주절) to be loved by her fans. (종속절)

(4) a. It is likely (주절) that she will qualify for the LPGA. (종속절)

b. She is likely (주절) to qualify for the LPGA. (종속절)

(5) a. It is certain (주절) that she will debut in the LPGA this year. (종속절)

b. She is certain (주절) to debut in the LPGA this year. (종속절)

(6) a. It is anticipated (주절) that she will hit a birdie during the first round. (종속절)

b. She is anticipated (주절) to hit a birdie during the first round. (종속절)

(7) a. It was reported (주절) that she had hit an eagle during the final round. (종속절)

b. She was reported (주절) to have hit an eagle during the final round. (종속절)

(8) a. It turned out (주절) that she had hit the highest score in the LPGA. (종속절)

b. She turned out (주절) to have hit the highest score in the LPGA. (종속절)

(9) a. It proved (주절) that she was a better golfer than the previous year's LPGA champion. (종속절)

b. She proved (주절) to be a better golfer than the previous year's LPGA champion. (종속절)

(10) a. It is estimated (주절) that the cash prize will amount to one million dollars. (종속절)

b. The cash prize is estimated (주절) to amount to one million dollars. (종속절)

Special Tips on Subject-to-Subject Raising

1. a. It seems (주절) that John is a billionaire. (종속절(명제))

   b. John seems (주절) to be a billionaire. (종속절(명제))

In sentence (1a), the verb *seems* is a one-place predicate. It selects the embedded clause *that John is a billionaire* as a proposition. In sentence (1b), the subject of the embedded clause, *John*, undergoes movement to the main clause subject position. This is a so-called subject-to-subject raising. Subject-to-subject raising is possible when the predicate of the main clause is a one-place predicates that selects a proposition.

2. One-place Predicates with Propositions

   (1) certain (~이 확실하다)

   (2) likely

   (3) unlikely

   (4) sure (~이 확실하다)

   (5) seem

   (6) prove

   (7) turn out

   (8) happen

   (9) appear

Subject-to-subject raising is also possible when the predicate of the main clause is a passive derived from a two-place predicate transitive verb.

3. a. It is expected　　that Sue will make a good wife for Harry.
주절　　종속절(명제)

b. Sue is expected　　to make a good wife for Harry.
주절　　종속절(명제)

In sentence (3a) the predicate *expected* is a passive verb derived from the two-place predicate transitive verb *expect*. In sentence (3b) the subject of the embedded clause, *Sue*, undergoes movement to the main clause subject position. This is an example of subject-to-subject raising. Therefore, subject-to-subject raising is also possible when the predicate of the main clause is a passive verb derived from a two-place predicate transitive verb. The following verbs are examples of passive verbs derived from the two-place predicate transitive verbs. These should also be regarded as one-place predicates with propositions.

4. Passive verbs derived from two-place predicate transitive verbs

(1) believed

(2) expected

(3) thought

(4) alleged

(5) supposed

(6) reported

(7) said

(8) assumed

(9) suspected

Dialogue 2

Tony : Hello, ladies! I have a feeling you are gossiping as usual, right? What's the word?

Jane : Haha, you know us too well. Well, you know Bob Smith's new wife, Janet? It was thought that she was a beauty in her school days, but apparently it's all plastic surgery!

Tony : Oh dear, she was thought to be a beauty, wasn't she? Still, it is said that Bob himself was the most handsome guy in his hometown.

Jina : True, Bob is said to be the most handsome guy in his hometown, but after that horrible industrial accident, there are only three men left in the town!

Jane : You don't say! Wow, did they ever catch the one responsible for the accident?

Jina : It is supposed that Homer Simpson is the culprit, but the company president denies it.

Tony : Well, we all know that the president is suspected to be a liar. From what everybody is saying, Homer Simpson is supposed to be the one responsible.

Jane : Honestly, I just don't care whether it is suspected that the president is a liar. Boring! Ladies, you will never believe what I read in the paper today. It is reported in the Town Gazette that most dentists are secret supporters of the candy industry. Imagine that!

Jina : Most dentists are reported to be secret supporters of the candy industry?! What a scandal!

Tony : Oh my goodness. What is this world coming to?

Q. 위 대화문에서 종속절의 주어가 주절의 주어로 이동하는 예를 보이지 않는 술어는 무엇인가?

① thought ② said ③ supposed ④ reported ⑤ coming

정답 : ⑤

Exercise 1

보기에 주어진 패턴대로 문장을 변형시키시오.

Ex

1. a. It is likely (주절) that Janet **will set** a new world record in weight lifting. (종속절)

   b. Janet is likely (주절) **to set** a new world record in weight lifting. (종속절)

2. a. It was almost certain (주절) that the senator **would lose** the next election. (종속절)

   b. The senator was almost certain (주절) **to lose** the next election. (종속절)

(1) a. It was unlikely that Jack and Jill would break up.

b. Jack and Jill were unlikely (   ) (   ).

(2) a. It is likely that there will be a storm soon.

b. (   ) is likely (   ) (   ) a storm soon.

보기에 주어진 패턴대로 문장을 변형시키시오.

Ex

1. a. It is said (주절) that Mr. Smith **is** the best driver in his hometown. (종속절)

   b. Mr. Smith is said (주절) **to be** the best driver in his hometown. (종속절)

2. a. It is reported (주절) that most dentists **were** secret supporters of the candy industry. (종속절)

   b. Most dentists are reported (주절) **to have been** secret supporters of the candy industry. (종속절)

(3) a. It was believed that the island was uninhabited.

b. The island was believed (   ) (   ) uninhabited.

(4) a. It is thought that Mrs. Jensen was a beauty when young.

b. Mrs. Jensen is thought (   ) (   ) (   ) a beauty when young.

보기에 주어진 패턴대로 문장을 변형시키시오.

Ex 1. a. Was it likely (주절) that the game would end in a tie? (종속절)

b. Was the game likely (주절) to end in a tie? (종속절)

(5) a. Is it likely that she will arrive on time?

b. Is (   ) likely (   ) (   ) on time?

(6) a. Isn't it likely that the hooligans will admit their mistakes?

b. (   ) the hooligans likely (   ) (   ) their mistakes?

(7) a. Is it said that she is the best golfer in the States?

b. Is (   ) said (   ) (   ) the best golfer in the States?

(8) a. Is it alleged that he was a swindler when young?

b. Is (   ) alleged (   ) (   ) (   ) a swindler when young?

Wrap Up

종속절 주어 ➡ 주절의 주어

- One-place Predicate Sentence with Proposition

(1) a. Comp + Expl + Tense + Neg + Link + Aspect + Predicate-1 +

주절

Comp + Sub + Tense + Neg + Link + Aspect + Predicate

종속절(명제)

b. Comp + Subj + Tense + Neg + Link + Aspect + Predicate-1 +

수절

( ) + ( ) + ( ) + Neg + Link + Aspect + Predicate

종속절(명제)

One-place Predicates with Propositions

- Adjectives
  - (1) certain
  - (2) likely
  - (3) unlikely
  - (4) sure

- Verbs
  - (1) seem
  - (2) prove
  - (3) turn out
  - (4) happen
  - (5) appear

- Passive verbs
  - (1) believed
  - (2) expected
  - (3) thought
  - (4) alleged
  - (5) supposed
  - (6) reported
  - (7) said
  - (8) assumed
  - (9) suspected

UNIT 12 무거운 주어와 목적어를 어떻게 할까?

What am I supposed to do with heavy subjects and objects?

Warm Up

문장을 구성하는 기본 문장 성분은 Comp, Subject, Tense, Neg, Link, Aspect, Predicate입니다. 술어가 1가 술어인 경우는 주어(subject)나 명제(proposition)와 같은 하나의 문장성분이 필요하며, 2가 술어 또는 3가 술어인 경우는 주어 외에도 문장성분이 하나 또는 두 개 더 필요합니다.

문장성분 중에서 주어나 목적어는 대부분 명사구(noun phrase), 복합명사구(complex noun phrase) 또는 절(clause)입니다. 복합명사구는 자체 내에 절(clause)이나 전치사구(prepositional phrase)가 들어 있는 명사구를 의미합니다.

주어가 복합명사구이거나 절인 경우 주어는 무거운 주어(heavy subject)로 간주됩니다. 목적어가 복합명사구이거나 절인 경우도 무거운 목적어(heavy object)로 분류됩니다. 문장에 무거운 주어나 목적어가 있을 경우 문장의 균형을 위해서 변화를 줄 수 있습니다.

1. 주어가 절인 경우

- **주어를 문장의 맨 끝으로 이동시킨 후 가주어(expletive)를 사용한다.**

a. Subj + Tense + Pred-2 + Obj →

b. It + Tense + Pred-2 + Obj + Subj

Ex a. That a 22-year old was crowned Miss Korea (Subj) surprises (Pred-2) people (Obj).

b. It (Expl) surprises (Pred-2) people (Obj) that a 22-year old was crowned Miss Korea (Subj).

2. 주어가 복합명사구인 경우

- 주어내의 절을 문장의 맨 끝으로 이동시킨다.

a. Subj + Tense + Pred-1 ➡

b. Subj + Tense + Pred-1 + Clause

Ex a. The news that Miss Korea 2012 will compete in Miss Universe 2013 (Subj) was (Tense) announced (Pred-1).

b. The news (Subj) was (Tense) announced (Pred-1) that Miss Korea 2012 will compete in Miss Universe 2013 (Clause).

3. 목적어가 절인 경우

- 목적어를 문장의 맨 끝으로 이동시킨 가목적어(expletive)를 사용한다.

  a. Subj + Tense + Pred-3 + Obj + OC ➡

  b. Subj + Tense + Pred-3 + it + OC + Obj

Ex

a. You (Subj) should (Tense) make (Pred-3) that you cannot tolerate his aggressive behavior (Heavy Object) clear (OC).

b. You (Subj) should (Tense) make (Pred-3) it (Ex) clear (OC) that you cannot tolerate his aggressive behavior (Object).

4. 목적어가 복합명사구인 경우

- 목적어내의 절을 문장의 맨 끝으로 이동시킨다.

a. Subj + Tense + Pred-3 + DO + IO ➡

b. Subj + Tense + Pred-3 + DO + IO + Clause

Ex

a. He (Subj) announced (Pred-3) the new policy that the salary step system would be replaced with an annual pay system (DO) to all the employees (IO).

b. He (Subj) announced (Pred-3) the new policy (DO) to all the employees (IO) that the salary step system would be replaced with an annual pay system (DO).

- 목적어 전체를 문장의 맨 끝으로 이동시킨다.

a. Subj + Tense + Pred-3 + DO + IO ➡

b. Subj + Tense + Pred-3 + + IO + DO

Ex

a. Korea (Subj) dispatched (Pred-3) a total of 240 athletes to compete in 22 events (DO) to London (IO).

b. Korea (Subj) dispatched (Pred-3) to London (IO) a total of 240 athletes to compete in 22 events (DO).

Qviz 1

다음 보기에 주어진 문장을 살펴보고 물음에 답하시오.

Ex

1. a. That lawmakers are not reliable makes me feel upset.
   b. It makes me feel upset that lawmakers are not reliable.

2. a. That new employees complain about their pay surprises the boss.
   b. It surprises the boss that new employees complain about their pay.

3. a. That John does not clean his room makes his wife angry.
   b. It makes his wife angry that John does not clean his room.

1. 위 보기에 주어진 a형 문장들(1a, 2a, 3a)의 공통점은 무엇인가?

① 주어가 절(clause)로 되어 있다.
② 주어가 명사구(noun phrase)로 되어 있다.
③ 목적어가 절(clause)로 되어 있다.
④ 목적어가 명사구(noun phrase)로 되어 있다.

2. 위 보기에 주어진 b형 문장들(1b, 2b, 3b)이 a형 문장들(1a, 2a, 3a) 보다 더 균형 있는 문장이라면 그 이유는 무엇인가?

① 가주어(expletive)가 있다.
② 가목적어(expletive)가 있다.
③ 무거운 주어가 문장의 끝에 있다.
④ 무거운 목적어가 문장의 끝에 있다.

Quiz 2

다음 보기에 주어진 문장을 살펴보고 물음에 답하시오.

Ex

1\. a. The thought that she might be a detective occurred to me.

b. The thought occurred to me that she might be a detective.

2\. a. The time to decorate the house for the party has come.

b. The time has come to decorate the house for the party.

3\. a. Permission for the captive to leave was granted.

b. Permission was granted for the captive to leave.

1\. 위 보기에 주어진 a형 문장들(1a, 2a, 3a)의 공통점은 무엇인가?

① 주어가 복합명사구(complex noun phrase)로 되어 있다.

② 주어가 절(clause)로 되어 있다.

③ 목적어가 복합명사구(complex noun phrase)로 되어 있다.

④ 목적어가 질(clause)로 되어 있다.

2\. 위 보기에 주어진 b형 문장들(1b, 2b, 3b)이 a형 문장들(1a, 2a, 3a) 보다 더 균형 있는 문장이라면 그 이유는 무엇인가?

① 주어가 가벼워졌다.

② 주어가 무거워졌다.

③ 목적어가 가벼워졌다.

④ 목적어가 무거워졌다.

Quiz 3

다음 보기에 주어진 문장을 살펴보고 물음에 답하시오.

Ex

1. a. He read a manual for the new Japanese-made washing machine yesterday.
   b. He read a manual yesterday for the new Japanese-made washing machine.

2. a. She came across the man who she had dated while in college yesterday.
   b. She came across the man yesterday who she had dated in college.

3. a. Jina made her intention to marry the self-made man clear.
   b. Jina made her intention clear to marry the self-made man.

1. 위 보기에 주어진 a형 문장들(1a, 2a, 3a)의 공통점은 무엇인가?

(1) 주어가 복합명사구(complex noun phrase)로 되어 있다.

(2) 주어가 절(clause)로 되어 있다.

(3) 목적어가 복합명사구(complex noun phrase)로 되어 있다.

(4) 목적어가 절(clause)로 되어 있다.

2. 위 보기에 주어진 b형 문장들(1b, 2b, 3b)이 a형 문장들(1a, 2a, 3a)보다 더 균형 있는 문장이라면 그 이유는 무엇인가?

(1) 주어가 가벼워졌다.

(2) 주어가 무거워졌다.

(3) 목적어가 가벼워졌다.

(4) 목적어가 무거워졌다.

Lecture 1

주어가 절인 경우

- 주어를 문장의 맨 끝으로 이동시킨 후 가주어 사용

  a. Subj + Tense + Pred-2 + Obj ➡

  b. It + Tense + Pred-2 + Obj + Subj

Ex

a. That a 22-year old was crowned Miss Korea (Subj) surprises (Pred-2) people (Obj).

b. **It** (Expl) surprises (Pred-2) people (Obj) that a 22-year old was crowned Miss Korea (Subj).

주어가 복합명사구인 경우

- 주어내의 절을 문장의 맨 끝으로 이동시킨다.

  a. Subj + Tense + Pred-1 ➡

  b. Subj + Tense + Pred-1 + Clause

Ex

a. The news that Miss Korea 2012 will compete in Miss Universe 2013 (Subject) was (Tense) announced (Pred-1).

b. The news (Subject) was (Tense) announced (Pred-1) that Miss Korea 2012 will compete in Miss Universe 2013 (Clause).

Sentence Analysis

(1) a.

That China is rising to power	has	drawn	international interest and attention.
Subj	Tense	Pred-2	Obj

b.

It	has	drawn	international interest and attention	that China is rising to power.
Expl	Tense	Pred-2	Obj	Subj

(2) a.

That China is the biggest creditor nation	contrasts with	the economic demotion of the USA.
Subj	Pred-2	Obj

b.

It	contrasts with	the economic demotion of the USA	that China is the biggest creditor nation.
Expl	Pred-2	Obj	Subj

(3) a.

For the USA to come up with a new Asian strategy	is	necessary.
Subj	Tense	Pred-1

b.

It	is	necessary	for the USA to come up with a new Asian strategy.
Expl	Tense	Pred-1	Subj

(4) a.

That he would visit Asian countries	relates to	China's rise to power.
Subj	Pred-2	Obj

b.

It	relates to	China's rise to power	that he would visit Asian countries.
Expl	Pred-2	Obj	Subj

(5) a.

That he will present a new foreign policy toward Asia	is	evident.
Subj	Tense	Pred-1

b.

It	is	evident	that he will present a new foreign policy toward Asia.
Expl	Tense	Pred-1	Subj

(6) a. That the new Japanese government wants to review its alliance with the USA (Subj)

will (Tense) alter (Pred-2) the influence of the USA on Asia (Obj).

b. It (Expl) will (Tense) alter (Pred-2) the influence of the USA on Asia (Obj)

that the new Japanese government wants to review its alliance with the USA (Subj).

(7) a. That China is rising to power (Subj) is (Tense) troubling (Pred-2) the American President (Obj).

b. It (Expl) is (Tense) troubling (Pred-2) the American President (Obj) that China is rising to power (Subj).

(8) a. That the Prime Minister has proposed an East Asian community (Subj) has (Tense) triggered (Pred-2)

conflict between the two countries (Obj).

b. It (Expl) has (Tense) triggered (Pred-2) conflict between the two countries (Obj)

that the Prime Minister has proposed an East Asian community (Subj).

(9) a. That the Obama administration has developed cooperative relations with Asia

Subj

is | beneficial | to fix a trade dispute.

Tense | Pred-1 | Mod

b. It | is | beneficial | to fix a trade dispute

Expl | Tense | Pred-1 | Mod

that the Obama administration has developed cooperative relations with Asia.

Subj

(10) a. That the Japanese government terminates its Indian Ocean refueling agreement

Subj

for American warships | has | evoked | a tension between the two countries.

Tense | Pred-2 | Obj

b. It | has | evoked | a tension between the two countries | that the Japanese

Expl | Tense | Pred-2 | Obj

government terminates its Indian Ocean refueling agreement for American warships.

Subj

Special Tips on Balance of Sentence Structure

Balance of Sentence Structure

When the subject in a sentence is a clause or a complex noun phrase, the sentence might be regarded as an unbalanced sentence. We can alter these sentences to have more balanced sentence structures.

1. a. That Korea scored fourth in the 2012 London Olympics surprises people.

   Subj / Pred-2 / Obj

   b. It surprises people that Korea scored fourth in the 2012 London Olympics.

   Expl / Pred-2 / Obj / Subj

Sentence (1a) is comprised of a subject, two-place predicate, and object. The subject is a clause and this leads to the unbalance of the sentence. Displacing the clausal subject to the sentence final position, such as in (1b), gives the sentence a more balanced structure.

2. a. The news that Miss Korea 2012 will compete in Miss Universe 2013

   Subject

   was announced.

   Tense / Pred-1

   b. The news was announced

   Subject / Tense / Pred-1

   that Miss Korea 2012 will compete in Miss Universe 2013.

   Clause

Sentence (2a) has a complex noun phrase subject and this leads to the unbalance structure of the sentence. Displacement of the complex noun phrase-internal clause to the sentence-final position such as in (2b) gives the sentence a more balanced structure.

Dialogue 1

Harry : Good morning, and welcome to the teachers' meeting. Does anybody have any issues to raise?

Judy : Actually I do. There seems to have been some errors made in the calculation of the statistics on grades this semester. That the statistics are not reliable bothers me.

Harry : Well, as chair of the faculty committee, I admit it also bothers me that the statistics are not reliable. I will look into the matter personally. Anything else?

Judy: Yes. Mr. Jeeter, the facilities manager, has informed me that it angers the janitors that people smoke in the teachers' restrooms. I am a nonsmoker, So I don't smoke. And the fact that teachers smoke in there angers me as well.

Harry : That people are smoking the teachers' restrooms angers a lot of people, but what can we do about it? It is illegal to use surveillance cameras in public restrooms.

Judy : It's a good point. Well, how about using sniffer dogs?

Harry : Hmmm... I will have my assistant look into that. Now if that is all, this meeting is adjourned.

Judy : See you next week.

Q. 위 대화문에서 무거운 주어를 해결하기 위해서 사용하고 있는 두 가지 방법은?

① 주어를 문장의 끝으로 이동시킨다.
② 주어를 절에서 명사구로 바꾼다.
③ 주어를 두 부분으로 분리시킨다.
④ 주어를 시제절에서 비시제절로 바꾼다.

정답 : ①, ②

Exercise 1

1. 다음 보기에 주어진 문장들의 상관관계를 잘 이해하고 이와 비슷한 패턴이 되도록 주어진 문장을 변형시키시오.

> Ex
>
> a. **That the U.S. influence on the global economy** is weakening seems probable.
>
> b. It seems probable **that the U.S. influence on the global economy is weakening.**

(1) a. That the world is witnessing a power shift from the West towards Asia worries a superpower.

b. (　　　　　) (　　　　　) a superpower that the world is witnessing a power shift from the West to Asia.

(2) a. That Washington has reaffirmed its commitment to security in the Asia-Pacific region is worth noting.

b. (　　　　　) (　　　　　) (　　　　　) noting that Washington has reaffirmed its commitment to security in the Asia-Pacific region.

2. 다음 보기에 주어진 문장들의 상관관계를 잘 이해하고 이와 비슷한 패턴이 되도록 주어진 문장을 변형시키시오.

> Ex
>
> a. **To hammer out a new Asian strategy** seems imminent.
>
> b. It seems imminent **to hammer out a new Asian strategy.**

(1) a. For the two traditional allies to map out a more effective win-win strategy is important.

b. (   ) (   ) (   ) for the two traditional allies to map out a more effective win-win strategy.

(2) a. To attend the speech through a random selection process was not easy.

b. (   ) (   ) (   ) (   ) to attend the speech through a random selection process

3. 다음 보기에 주어진 문장들의 상관관계를 잘 이해하고 이와 비슷한 패턴이 되도록 주어진 문장을 변형시키시오.

> Ex
> a. Is where the accident happened not fully clear?
> b. Is it not fully clear where the accident happened?

(1) a. Is why HUFS was chosen for Obama's speech not fully clear yet?

b. (   ) (   ) not fully clear yet why HUFS was chosen for Obama's speech?

(2) a. Does how the White House selected HUFS really matter?

b. (   ) (   ) really matter how the White House selected HUFS?

4. 다음 보기에 주어진 문장들의 상관관계를 잘 이해하고 이와 비슷한 패턴이 되도록 주어진 문장을 변형시키시오.

Ex

a. **The thought that the U.S. President would visit Korea** occurred to college students.

b. **The thought** occurred to college students **that the U.S. President would visit Korea.**

(1) a. Many students **who have defected from the North** are enrolled at HUFS.

b. Many students are enrolled at HUFS ( ) ( ) ( ) ( ) **the North.**

(2) a. The time **to unify North and South Korea** has come.

b. The time has come ( ) ( ) North and South Korea.

Coffee Break

시제와 언어

지구상에 많은 언어가 존재합니다. 지구상에 존재하는 많은 언어를 시제가 나타나는 방법의 관점에서 분류했을 때 크게 세가지로 분류할 수 있습니다. 첫 번째는 시제를 나타내기 위해서 단어가 첨가되는 언어가 있습니다. 대표적인 언어가 중국어입니다. 중국어에서는 과거시제를 나타내기 위해서 단어가 첨가됩니다.

我(워)爱(아이)你(니) ➡ 我(워)爱(아이)过(꿔)你(니)

"我(워)爱(아이)你(니)"는 '나는 너를 사랑한다'의 의미인 중국어표현으로서 세 단어로 되어있는 문장입니다. "我(워)爱(아이)你(니)"를 과거시제 즉 '나는 너를 사랑했다'로 변화시키려면 과거를 나타내는 단어 "过(꿔)"를 첨가하면 됩니다. 중국어처럼 단어를 첨가해서 시제를 나타내는 언어를 고립어라고 합니다.

시제를 나타내기 위해서 단어를 첨가하는 언어도 있지만 음절을 첨가하는 언어가 있습니다. 대표적인 언어가 한국어입니다. 한국어에서는 과거시제를 나타내기 위해 음절을 첨가합니다.

먹다 ➡ 먹었다

'먹다"를 과거시제로 바꾸려면 과거를 나타내는 음절형태소 "었"을 첨가합니다. "었"은 하나의 단어를 형성하지는 못하지만 하나의 음절을 형성합니다. 한국어처럼 시제를 나타내기 위해서 음절형태소를 첨가하는 언어를 교착어라고 합니다.

시제를 나타내기 위해서 단어를 첨가하는 언어도 있고 음절을 첨가하는 언어도 있지만 단어도 아니고 음절도 아닌 형태소를 첨가하는 언어가 있습니다. 대표적인 언어가 영어입니다.

kiss ➡ kissed

kiss를 과거로 변화시키려면 과거를 나타내는 'ed'를 첨가합니다. 'ed'는 단어도 아니고 하나의 음절도 형성하지 않습니다. 영어처럼 시제를 나타내기 위해서 단어도 아니고 음절도 아닌 형태소를 참가하는 언어를 굴절어라고 합니다.

Quiz. 영어는 시제를 나타내는 방법에 있어서 굴절어로 분류된다. 하지만 영어가 중국어처럼 고립에 의해서 시제를 나타내는 경우도 있다. 다음 문장에서 고립에 의해서 시제가 나타나는 경우는?

① John likes her　　② He will get a job
③ Be quiet　　④ She smiles

정답 : ②

Lecture 2

목적어가 절인 경우

- 목적어를 문장의 맨 끝으로 이동시킨 후 가목적어를 사용한다.

a. Subj + Tense + Pred-3 + Obj + OC →

b. Subj + Tense + Pred-3 + it + OC + Obj

Ex

a. You	should	make	that you cannot tolerate his aggressive behavior	clear.
Subj	Tense	Pred-3	Obj	OC

b. You	should	make	it	clear	that you cannot tolerate his aggressive behavior.
Subj	Tense	Pred-3	Expl	OC	Obj

Sentence Analysis

(1)

a. Queen Elizabeth II	officially	declared	the Olympics	open.
Sub	Mod	Pred-3	Obj	OC

b. The judges	did	not	make	why the athlete was disqualified	clear.
Sub	Tense	Neg	Pred-3	Obj	OC

c. The judges	did	not	make	it	clear	why the athlete was disqualified.
Sub	Tense	Neg	Pred-3	Expl	OC	Obj

(2) a.

The judge	declared	him	the winner.
Sub	Pred-3	Obj	OC

b.

We	should	make	that we cannot accept the ruling	clear.
Sub	Tense	Pred-3	Obj	OC

c.

We	should	make	it	clear	that we cannot accept the ruling.
Sub	Tense	Pred-3	Expl	OC	Obj

(3) a*.

The IOC	should	take	to settle conflicts and tension	upon itself.
Subj	Tense	Pred-2	Obj	

b.

The IOC	should	take	it	upon itself	to settle conflicts and tension.
Subj	Tense	Pred-2	Expl		Obj

c.

They	should	bear	it	in mind	that athletes should have the true spirit of sportsmanship.
Subj	Tense	Pred-2	Expl		Obj

(4) a.

We	should	make	that we have objections against the unfair action	officially known.
Subject	Tense	Pred-3	Object	OC

b.

We	should	make	it	officially known	that we have objections against the unfair action.
Subject	Tense	Pred-3	Expl	OC	Object

목적어가 절인 경우

- 목적어가 복합명사구인 경우

① a. Subj + Tense + Pred-3 + O + OC ➡

b. Subj + Tense + Pred-3 + O + OC + Clause

② a. Subj + Tense + Pred-3 + DO + IO ➡

b. Subj + Tense + Pred-3 + + IO + DO

Sentence Analysis

(1) a. A boss (Subj) mentioned (Pred-3) the possibility that the pay system might be changed (DO)

to his employees. (IO)

b. He (Subj) announced (Pred-3) the new pay policy (DO) to the employees (IO)

that the salary step system would be replaced with an annual pay system. (Clause)

c. He (Subj) also (Mod) announced (Pred-3) to the employees (IO)

another policy that employees would not receive a stipend for unused annual leave. (DO)

(2) a. The employees / protested / the company's new plan to introduce a performance-based pay system / very strongly.

Subj / Pred-2 / Obj / Mod

b. The senior employees / protested / the company's new plan / very strongly / that introduces a performance-based pay system.

Subj / Pred-2 / Obj / Mod / Clause

c. The junior employees / welcomed / impassionately. / the company's new plan to introduce a performance-based pay system.

Subj / Pred-2 / Mod / Obj

(3) a. Korean citizens / regard / the traffic congestion charges which are levied against the owners of department stores and shopping malls / as a solution.

Subj / Pred-3 / Obj / OC

b. Korean citizens / regard / the traffic congestion charges / as a solution / which are levied against the owners of shopping malls.

Subj / Pred-3 / Obj / OC / Clause

c. Korean citizens / regard / as a solution for traffic jams / the traffic congestion charge which are levied against the owners of department stores and shopping malls.

Subj / Pred-3 / OC / Obj

(4) a. Students do not take the high tuition fees which are imposed on their parents into consideration.

Subj / Tense / Neg / Pred-2 / Obj

b. Students do not take the high tuition fees into consideration which ares imposed on their parents.

Subj / Tense / Neg / Pred-2 / Obj / Clause

c. Students do not take into consideration the high tuition fees which are imposed on their parents.

Subj / Tense / Neg / Pred-2 / Obj

Special Tips on Balance of Sentence Structure

Balance of Sentence Structure

When the object in a sentence is a clause or a complex noun phrase that contains a clause, the sentence might be regarded as an unbalanced sentence. We can transform these sentences to have more balanced sentence structures.

1. a.

We	should	make	that we cannot accept an annual salary system	clear.
Sub	Tense	Pred-3	Obj	OC

b.

We	should	make	it	clear	that we cannot accept an annual salary system.
Sub	Tense	Pred-3	Expl	OC	Obj

Sentence (1a) is comprised of a subject, three-place predicate, object, and object complement. The object is a clause and this leads to the unbalance of the sentence. A solution is displacing the clausal object to the sentence final position and substituting dummy subject *it* in the base position such as in (1b). This transformation makes the sentence have a more balanced sentence structure.

2. a.

A new CEO	announced	the new policy that the salary step system would be replaced with an annual salary system	to the employees.
Subj	Pred-3	DO	IO

b. A new CEO announced the new policy to the employees
Subj / Pred-3 / DO / IO

that that salary step system would be replaced with an annual salary system.
Clause

c. A new CEO announced to the employees a new policy that the
Subj / Pred-3 / IO

salary step system would be replaced with an annual salary system.
DO

Sentence (2a) is comprised of a subject, three-place predicate, direct object, and indirect object. The object is a complex noun phrase that contains a clause, and this leads to the unbalance of the sentence. One solution is displacing the complex noun phrase-internal clause to the sentence final position such as in (2b). This transformation makes the sentence have a more balanced sentence structure. Another solution is to move the whole object to the sentence final position as in (2c). This transformation also makes the sentence have a more balanced structure.

Dialogue 2

Jimmy : Guess what, Jimmy? The time to decorate the house for Christmas has come at last.

Tony : The time has come to deck the halls? That's terrific!

Jimmy : I appreciate your enthusiasm. You know, the thought occurred to me that we might need some new lights.

Tony : The thought that we might need some new lights occurred to me a long time ago, Dad. Can we go out and get some today?

Jimmy : Sure, but I want to save money on decorations this year clear.

Tony : Okay, Dad. You have made your intention clear to save money. Crystal clear. Now can we go?!

Jimmy : Not yet. Permission for us to leave was granted by your mother, but only on the condition that we tidy up the house first.

Tony : Permission was granted for us to leave, but we have to clean first?

Jimmy : Affirmative.

Tony : OK, I'll take care of my room, and you clean everything else!

Q. 위 대화문에서 무거운 주어나 목적어를 해결하기 위해서 사용하고 있는 방법은?

① 주어나 목적어를 문장의 끝으로 이동시킨다.

② 주어나 목적어를 두 부분으로 분리시킨다.

③ 주어나 목적어를 시제절에서 비시제절로 바꾼다.

④ 주어나 목적어를 절에서 명사구로 바꾼다.

정답 : ②

Exercise 1

1. 다음 보기에 주어진 문장들의 상관관계를 잘 이해하고 이와 비슷한 패턴이 되도록 주어진 문장을 변형시켜 보세요.

> Ex 1. a. John did not make why he had to leave so early clear.
> b. John did not make it clear why he had to leave so early.

(1) a. The judges did not make why the athlete was disqualified clearly understood.
b. The judges did not make (   ) (   ) (   ) why the athlete was disqualified.

(2) a. Napoleon did not give that he might be defeated at Waterloo a thought.
b. Napoleon did not give (   ) (   ) (   ) that he might be defeated at Waterloo.

(3) a*. I thought to find fault with him useless.
b. I thought (   ) (   ) to find fault with him.

(4) a*. We found to cope with the problem very difficult.
b. We found (   ) (   ) (   ) to cope with the problem.

2. 다음 보기에 주어진 문장들의 상관관계를 잘 이해하고 이와 비슷한 패턴이 되도록 주어진 문장을 변형시켜 보세요.

> Ex 1. a. He drank the tea that his wife had brought from China every morning.
> b. He drank the tea every morning that his wife had brought from China.

(1) a. The master of ceremonies introduced a famous musician who had flown in from New York to the audience.

b. The master of ceremonies introduced a famous musician to the audience ( ) ( ) ( ) ( ) from New York.

(2) a. The boss mentioned the possibility that she might get a promotion yesterday.

b. The boss mentioned the possibility yesterday ( ) ( ) ( ) ( ) ( ) ( ).

(3) a. She made her intention not to receive the prize from the committee clear.

b. She made her intention clear ( ) ( ) ( ) ( ) ( ) ( ) ( ) ( ).

(4) a. We welcomed the athletes who had participated in the London Olympics at the airport.

b. We welcomed the athletes at the airport ( ) ( ) ( ) in the London Olympics.

3. 다음 보기에 주어진 문장들의 상관관계를 잘 이해하고 이와 비슷한 패턴이 되도록 주어진 문장을 변형 시켜 보세요

> Ex 1. a. He drank the sweet-smelling tea that his wife had brought from China every morning.
>
> b. He drank every morning the sweet-smelling tea that his wife had brought from China.

(1) a. Korea dispatched a total of 240 athletes to compete in 22 events to London.

b. Korea dispatched ( ) ( ) a total of 240 athletes to compete in 22 events.

(2) a. The IOC awarded a total of 13 gold medals, 8 silver medals, and 7 bronze medals to Korea.

b. The IOC awarded (   ) (   ) a total of 13 gold medals, 8 silver medals, and 7 bronze medals.

Wrap Up

문장의 균형을 위한 변형

● 주어가 절인 경우

· 주어를 문장의 맨 끝으로 이동시킨 후 가주어(expletive) 사용

a. Subj + Tense + Pred-2 + Obj →

b. It + Tense + Pred-2 + Obj + Subj

Ex

a. That a 22-year old was crowned Miss Korea (Subj) surprises (Pred-2) people (Obj).

b. It (Expl) surprises (Pred-2) people (Obj) that a 22-year old was crowned Miss Korea (Subj).

● 주어가 복합명사구인 경우

· 주어내의 절을 문장의 맨 끝으로 이동시킨다.

a. Subj + Tense + Pred-1 →

b. Subj + Tense + Pred-1 + Clause

Ex a. The news that Miss Korea 2012 will compete in Miss Universe 2013 (Subject) was (Tense) announced (Pred-1).

b. The news (Subject) was (Tense) announced (Pred-1) that Miss Korea 2012 will compete in Miss Universe 2013 (Clause).

● 목적어가 절인 경우

· 목적어를 문장의 끝으로 이동시킨 후 가목적어를 사용한다.

a. Subj + Tense + Pred-3 + Obj + OC →

b. Subj + Tense + Pred-3 + it + OC + Obj

Ex a. You (Subject) should (Tense) make (Pred-3) that you cannot tolerate his aggressive behavior (Heavy Object) clear (OC).

b. You (Subject) should (Tense) make (Pred-3) it (Expl) clear (OC) that you cannot tolerate his aggressive behavior (Heavy Object).

● 목적어가 복합명사구인 경우

· 목적어 내의 절을 문장의 끝으로 이동시킨다.

a. Subj + Tense + Pred-3 + DO + IO →

b. Subj + Tense + Pred-3 + DO + IO + Clause

Ex

a. He (Subj) announced (Pred-3) the policy that the salary step system would be replaced with an annual pay system (DO) to the employees (IO).

b. He (Subj) announced (Pred-3) the policy (DO) to the employees (IO) that the salary step system would be replaced with an annual pay system (Clause).

· 목적어 전체를 문장의 끝으로 이동시킨다.

a. Subj + Tense + Pred-3 + DO + IO ➡

b. Subj + Tense + Pred-3 + + IO + DO

Ex

a. He (Subj) announced (Pred-3) the policy that the salary step system would be replaced with an annual pay system (DO) to the employees (IO).

b. He (Subj) announced (Pred-3) to the employees (IO) the policy that the salary step system would be replaced with an annual pay system (DO).

UNIT 13 생략된 문장성분을 찾아서

Where are the missing sentence elements?

Warm Up

본 단원에서는 생략(ellipsis)에 대해서 다루도록 하겠습니다. 생략은 문장에서 두 번 이상 반복되는 요소를 생략하는 현상을 의미합니다. 두 번 이상 반복되는 요소를 생략하게 되면 문장의 잉여성이 살아지고 더 간결한 문장이 됩니다. 생략구문의 대표적인 예는 다음과 같습니다.

1. 술어의 생략

- a. Subj + Tense + Pred-1
  b. Subj + Tense + ______

Ex a. Jina has retired, but her husband has not retired yet.
b. Jina has retired, but her husband hasn't yet.

2. 술어와 수식어의 생략

- a. Subj + Tense + Pred-1 + Mod
  b. Subj + Tense + ______

- a. Jimmy works out every morning, and his wife works out every morning, too.
- b. Jimmy works out every morning, and his wife does, too.

3. 술어와 목적어의 생략

- a. Subj + Tense + Pred-2 + Obj
- b. Subj + Tense + ____________

- a. Jimmy likes outdoor sports, and his son likes outdoor sports, too.
- b. Jimmy likes outdoor sports, and his son does, too.

4. 술어, 목적어 그리고 장소의 생략

- a. Subj + Tense + Pred-3 + Obj + Loc
- b. Subj + Tense + __________________

- a. He ashes his cigarette in the ashtray because his wife asks him to ash his cigarette in the ashtray.
- b. He ashes his cigarette in the ashtray because his wife asks him to.

5. 술어, 목적어 그리고 소재의 생략

- a. Subj + Tense + Pred-3 + Obj + Substance

  b. Subj + Tense + ________________

Ex

a. She furnished her office with luxurious furniture though she was advised not to furnish her office with luxurious furniture.

b. She furnished her office with luxurious furniture though she was advised not to.

6. 술어, 직목, 간목, 수식어의 생략

- a. Subj + Tense + Pred-3 + DO + IO + Mod

  b. Subj + Tense + ________________

Ex

a. Sue wants to send the two sons to a foreign country for their education. However, her husband worries about money and does not want to send the two sons to a foreign country for their education.

b. Sue wants to send the two sons to a foreign country for their education. However, her husband worries about money and does not want to.

Quiz 1

다음 보기에 주어진 문장을 살펴보고 물음에 답하시오.

Ex

1. a. Sue smokes, but her sister doesn't smoke.
   b. Sue smokes, but her sister doesn't.
2. a. Harry works out every morning, and his wife works out every morning, too.
   b. Harry works out every morning, and his wife does, too.
3. a. John likes indoor sports, but Harry doesn't like indoor sports.
   b. John likes indoor sports, but Harry doesn't.

1. 위 보기에 주어진 1b의 문장에서 생략된 문장성분은?

   ① 술어와 목적어　　② 술어와 수식어　　③ 시제와 술어　　④ 술어

2. 위 보기에 주어진 2b의 문장에서 생략된 문장성분은?

   ① 술어와 목적어　　② 술어와 수식어　　③ 시제와 술어　　④ 술어

3. 위 보기에 주어진 3b의 문장에서 생략된 문장성분은?

   ① 술어와 목적어　　② 술어와 수식어　　③ 시제와 술어　　④ 술어

4. 2b에서 생략이 일어난 후 사용되는 조동사 does의 역할은 무엇인가?

   ① 보문어　　② 시제　　③ 부정어　　④ 강조

Quiz 2

다음 보기에 주어진 문장을 살펴보고 물음에 답하시오.

> Ex
> 1. a. Was she upset?
>   b. Yes, she was.
> 2. a. Is he kind to senior citizens?
>   b. No, he isn't.
> 3. a. Will you place the books on the desk?
>   b. Yes, I will.
> 4. a. Was he blamed for the mistake?
>   b. No, he wasn't. On the contrary he was praised for his achievements.

1. 위 보기에 주어진 1b의 문장에서 생략된 문장성분은?

① 술어와 목적어　② 술어와 수식어　③ 시제와 술어　④ 술어

2. 위 보기에 주어진 2b의 문장에서 생략된 문장성분은?

① 술어와 목적어　② 술어와 수식어　③ 시제와 술어　④ 술어

3. 위 보기에 주어진 3b의 문장에서 생략된 문장성분은?

① 술어와 목적어 그리고 장소　② 술어와 수식어
③ 시제와 술어　④ 술어

4. 위 보기에 주어진 4b의 문장에서 생략된 문장성분은?

① 술어와 목적어　② 술어와 수식어　③ 시제와 술어　④ 술어와 원인

Lecture 1

생략(ellipsis)

(1) a. Subj + Tense + Pred-1

b. Subj + Tense + ______

(2) a. Subj + Tense + Pred-1 + Mod

b. Subj + Tense + ____________

(3) a. Subj + Tense + Pred-2 + Obj + (Mod)

b. Subj + Tense + __________________

(4) a. Subj + Tense + Pred-3 + Obj + Loc

b. Subj + Tense + _________________

(5) a. Subj + Tense + Pred-3 + Obj + Substance

b. Subj + Tense + ______________________

(6) a. Subj + Tense + Pred-3 + Obj + Source

b . Subj + Tense + ___________________

Sentence Analysis

(1) a.

Sylvia	has	retired,	but	her husband	hasn't	retired	yet.
Subj	Tense	Pred-1	Conj	Subj	Tense	Pred-1	Mod

b.

Sylvia	has	retired,	but	her husband	hasn't	yet.
Subj	Tense	Pred-1	Conj	Subj	Tense	Mod

(2) a.

She	is	still	energetic,	and	her husband	is	still	energetic,	too.
Subj	Tense	Mod	Pred-1	Conj	Subj	Tense	Mod	Pred-1	

b.

She	is	still	energetic,	and	her husband	is,	too.
Subj	Tense	Mod	Pred-1	Conj	Subj	Tense	Mod

(3) a.

She	works out	regularly,	but	her husband	doesn't	work out	regularly.
Subj	Pred-1	Mod	Conj	Subj	Tense	Pred-1	Mod

b.

She	works out	regularly,	but	her husband	doesn't.
Subj	Pred-1	Mod	Conj	Subj	Tense

(4) a.

She	is	interested	in IT	though	her husband	isn't	interested	in IT	at all.
Subj	Tense	Pred-2	Obj	Comp	Subj	Tense	Pred-2	Obj	Mod

b.

She	is	interested	in IT	though	her husband	isn't	at all.
Subj	Tense	Pred-2	Obj	Comp	Subj	Tense	Mod

(5) a.

She	starts	a new business	although	her husband	wants	her not to start a new business.
Subj	Pred-2	Obj	Comp	Subj	Comp	Obj

b.

She	starts	a new business	although	her husband	wants	her not to.
Subj	Pred-2	Obj	Comp	Subj	Pred-2	Obj

(6) a. She located her office in downtown Seoul though she was advised not to locate her office in downtown Seoul.

She	located	her office	in downtown Seoul	though	she	was	advised	not to locate her office in downtown Seoul.
Subj	Pred-3	Obj	Loc	Comp	Subj	Tense	Pred-2	Obj

b. She located her office in downtown Seoul though she was advised not to.

She	located	her office	in downtown Seoul	though	she	was	advised	not to.
Subj	Pred-3	Obj	Loc	Comp	Subj	Tense	Pred-2	Obj

(7) a. She furnished her office with luxurious furniture though she was advised not to furnish her office with luxurious furniture.

She	furnished	her office	with luxurious furniture	though	she	was	advised	not to furnish her office with luxurious furniture.
Subj	Pred-3	Obj	Substance	Comp	Subj	Tense	Pred-2	Obj

b. She furnished her office with luxurious furniture though she was advised not to.

She	furnished	her office	with luxurious furniture	though	she	was	advised	not to.
Subj	Pred-3	Obj	Substance	Comp	Subj	Tense	Pred-2	Obj

(8) a. She went bankrupt quickly as her husband anticipated she would go bankrupt.

She	went bankrupt	quickly	as	her husband	anticipated	she would go bankrupt.
Subj	Pred-1	Mod	Comp	Subj	Pred-2	Obj

b. She went bankrupt quickly as her husband anticipated she would.

She	went bankrupt	quickly	as	her husband	anticipated	she would.
Subj	Pred-1	Mod	Comp	Subj	Pred-2	Obj

(9) a. She regrets that she had started the new business and she wishes she had not started the business.

Subj / Pred-2 / Obj / Conj / Subj / Pred-2 / Obj

b. She regrets that she had started the new business and she wishes she had not.

Subj / Pred-2 / Obj / Conj / Subj / Pred-2 / Obj

(10) a. He thinks that she should not have started the business.

Subj / Pred-2 / Obj

b. She also thinks that she should not have.

Subj / Mod / Pred-2 / Obj

(11) a. She wants to try a different business venture in the future.

Subj / Pred-2 / Obj

b. Coincidentally, he wants to as well.

Mod / Subj / Pred-2 / Obj / Mod

(12) a. She will borrow a lot of money from the bank.

Subj / Tense / Pred-3 / Obj / Source

b. Fortunately, he will not.

Mod / Subj / Tense / Neg

Special Tips on Ellipsis of Predicate Phrases and Tense Remnant

✓ Subj + Tense + Pred-1

✓ Subj + Tense + ___________

a. Jina has come back, but her husband has not come back yet.

b. Jina has come back, but her husband hasn't yet.

✓ Subj + Tense + Pred-1 + Mod

✓ Subj + Tense + ___________

a. Jmmy takes a walk every morning, and his wife takes a walk every morning, too.

b. Jimmy takes a walk every morning, and his wife does, too.

✓ Subj + Tense + Pred-2 + Obj

✓ Subj + Tense + ___________

a. Sue likes indoor sports, and her daughter likes indoor sports, too.

b. Jimmy likes indoor sports, and his son does, too.

✓ Subj + Tense + Link + Pred-3 + Obj + Loc

✓ Subj + Tense + Link + ___________

a. He hangs his coat in the closet because his wife wants him to hang his coat in the closet.

b. He hangs his coat in the closet because his wife wants him to.

When a predicate and the sentence elements that the predicate selects occur more than once in a sentence, they are omitted. When the predicate and the sentence elements that follow the predicate are omitted, Tense remains in tensed clauses and Link remains in infinitive clauses.

Dialogue 1

Bill : Did you hear the news about Sylvia?

Maria : You mean that she retired, but her husband hasn't retired yet?

Bill : Exactly. Sylvia has retired, but her husband hasn't yet. I really envy her!

Maria : I know, but I'm confused.

Bill : Why?

Maria : Because she's still energetic, and her husband is energetic, too. So why did she retire so soon?

Bill : Well, since she's still energetic and her husband is, too, I guess that means they'll have more time to travel together once he retires.

Maria : Yeah, maybe they can go climb mountains together or learn to sail.

Bill : That seems unlikely. Sylvia doesn't work out, but her husband does.

Maria : Oh, well, maybe now that she's retired, she'll have more time to work out.

Bill : You're right.

Q. 위 대화문에서 일어난 생략은 구체적으로 어떤 생략인가?

① 술어생략

② 술어와 수식어 생략

③ 술어와 목적어 생략

④ 시제 생략

정답 : ①

Exercise 1

다음 주어진 예문을 보고 물음에 답하시오.

Ex

1. a. He has come back, but she hasn't come back yet.
   b. He has come back, but she hasn't yet.

2. a. She is gorgeous, and her sister is gorgeous as well.
   b. She is gorgeous, and her sister is as well.

1. 문장 1b나 문장 2b가 문장 1a나 2a보다 더 나은 점이 있다면 무엇인가?

① 문장이 더 세련되어 있다.　　② 문장이 더 경제적이다.
③ 문장의 의미가 더 정확하다.　　④ 문장이 강조의 의미를 가지고 있다.

2. 문장 1b와 문장 2b에서 공통으로 생략된 부분은 무엇인가?

① 술어　② 술어와 수식어　③ 술어와 목적어　④ 술어와 주격보어

Exercise 2

다음 주어진 예문을 보고 물음에 답하시오.

> Ex
>
> 1. a. Brian does not eat after dinner, and his wife doesn't, either.
>   b. Kerry does not like sports, but his friend Jimmy does.
>
> 2. a. Tony moved to New York last year, and his brother Harry will, too.
>   b. Sue put her purse on the table, and so did her friend Jenny.

1. 보기에 주어진 문장 1a에서 생략된 부분은 무엇인가?

   ① eat ② after dinner ③ eat after dinner ④ do eating

2. 보기에 주어진 문장 1b에서 생략된 부분은 무엇인가?

   ① like ② sports ③ do sports ④ like sports

3. 문장 2a에서 생략된 부분은 무엇인가?

   ① move ② move to New York ③ last year ④ move to a some place

4. 문장 2b에서 생략된 부분은 무엇인가?

   ① put her purse on the table ② put her purse ③ put ④ on the table

Exercise 3

다음 주어진 예문을 보고 물음에 답하시오.

Ex Diana: I hear that you broke up with your boyfriend. Is that true?

Marian: Yes, it is (①). Things just didn't work out.

Diana: How come you broke up with him?

Marian: I just thought I should (②). I really had no choice.

Diana: Why?

Marian: I asked him to stop smoking, but he didn't (③).

Diana: Oh, wow. So he won't give up smoking. Is that the reason?

Marian: Yes. And he always sends text messages to someone else when we're on dates. I advised him not to (④), but he just ignored what I said.

Diana: Oh, I see. I guess you made a wise decision.

Marian: I think so too.

1. 위 dialogue의 빈칸 ①에 생략된 단어의 문장성분은 무엇인가?

① 술어 ② 술어 + 수식어 ③ 술어 + 목적어 ④ 술어 + 직목 + 간목 + 수식어

2. 위 dialogue의 빈칸 ②에 생략된 단어들의 문장성분은 무엇인가?

① 술어 ② 술어 + 수식어 ③ 술어 + 목적어 ④ 술어 + 직목 + 간목 + 수식어

3. 위 dialogue의 빈칸 ③에 생략된 단어들의 문장성분은 무엇인가?

① 술어 ② 술어 + 수식어 ③ 술어 + 목적어 ④ 술어 + 직목 + 간목 + 수식어

4. 위 dialogue의 빈칸 ④에 생략된 단어의 문장성분은 무엇인가?

① 술어 ② 술어 + 수식어 ③ 술어 + 목적어 ④ 술어 + 직목 + 간목 + 수식어

사용하면 안 좋은 표현들

지구상에 수 많은 국가와 민족이 존재한다. 서로 다른 국가와 민족은 서로 협력관계 속에서 살아감과 동시에 경쟁관계이므로 서로에 대한 언어적 표현이 항상 좋을 수 만은 없다. 민족과 민족 그리고 국가와 국가간의 대립관계는 각 국민을 칭하는 표현에 반영되어 있다. 다음 표현들을 살펴보자.

미국인: Yankee
캐나다인: Bluenose
영국인: John Bull
독일인: Hans
프랑스인: Frog

미국인을 지칭하는 표현 중에 "Yankee"라는 표현이 있다. 미국인을 왜 "Yankee"라고 부르는가에 대해서 여러 가지 설이 있지만 그 중에 하나는 미국이 영국으로부터 독립하기 위해서 치렀던 독립전쟁 당시 종종 불려졌던 "Yankee doodle dandy"라는 군가에서 유래되었다는 설이 유력하다.

캐나다인을 "Bluenose"라고 칭하는데 이는 캐나다인의 코가 추운 날씨 때문에 푸르스름한 데서 유래되었다고 한다. 영국인을 종종 "John Bull"이라고 부르는데 이는 영국인의 기질을 황소에 빗대어 나타낸 말이다. 독일인을 가리키는 표현 중에 "Hans"라는 표현이 있다. "Hans"는 영어 이름 "John"에 해당하는 독일어 이름으로서 독일인을 지칭하는 말로 사용된다.

프랑스인에 대해서 "Frog"라는 표현이 사용될 수 있다. 이는 프랑스인들이 개구리 요리를 먹는 데서 유래되었다고 한다. 이처럼 각 국가마다 국민들을 칭하는 고유한 표현들이 존재하는데, 이러한 표현들은 대부분 긍정적인 의미보다는 부정적인 의미를 가지고 있으므로 가능하면 사용하지 않는 것이 바람직하다.

Quiz. 다음 이름 중에서 미국정부를 상징하는 표현은?
① Ivan　② Uncle Sam　③ Chinois　④ Mr. Howdy doody

정답: ②

Lecture 2

생략(ellipsis)

(1) a. Subj + Tense + Pred-1

b. Subj + Tense + ______

(2) a. Subj + Tense + Pred-1 + Mod

b. Subj + Tense + ____________

(3) a. Subj + Tense + Pred-2 + Obj

b. Subj + Tense + ____________

(4) a. Subj + Tense + Pred-2 + Goal + Mod

b. Subj + Tense + ____________________

(5) a. Subj + Tense + Pred-2 + Cause

b. Subj + Tense + ______________

(6) a. Subj + Tense + Pred-3 + Object + Goal

b. Subj + Tense + ______________________

(7) a. Subj + Tense + Pred-3 + DO + IO + Mod

b. Subj + Tense + ________________________

Sentence Analysis

(1) a.

Tony	doesn't	work out,	and	he	is	very	fat.
Subj	Tense	Pred-1	Conj	Subj	Tense	Mod	Pred-1

b.

I	told	him	to work out,	but	I	am	not	sure	if he will.
Subj	Pred-3	IO	DO	Conj	Subj	Tense	Neg	Pred-1	Obj

(2) a.

He	is	a senior in high school,	but	he	doesn't	study	hard.
Subj	Pred-2	SC	Conj	Subj	Tense	Pred-1	Mod

b.

I	do	not	understand	why he doesn't.
Subj	Tense	Neg	Pred-2	Obj

(3) a.

He	plays	video games	excessively	in the evening.
Subj	Pred-2	Obj	Mod	Mod

b.

I	will	tell	him	not to,	but	I	am	not	sure	if he will listen to me.
Subj	Tense	Pred-2	IO	DO	Conj	Subj	Tense	Nog	Pred-2	Obj

(4) a.

He	often	sends	text messages	to his friends	during class.
Subj	Mod	Pred-3	DO	IO	Mod

b.

His homeroom teacher	is	angry	with him,	but	he	will	continue	to.
Subj	Tense	Pred-2	Obj	Conj	Subj	Tense	Pred-2	Obj

(5) a.

He	got	a bad score on the SAT,	but	has	applied to	one of the most prestigious universities.
Subj	Pred-2	Obj	Conj	Tense	Pred-2	Obj

b.

Unexpectedly,	his guidance counselor	allowed	him	to.
Mod	Subj	Pred-3	IO	DO

(6) a.

Tony's sister Jinny	is	going on a date	with an ex-convict.
Subj	Tense	Pred-2	Obj

b.

Her parents	don't	think	she should.
Subj	Tense	Pred-2	Obj

(7) a.

Jinny	wants	to go to UCLA for a language program.
Subj	Pred-2	Obj

b.

Her parents	are	not	well-off	and	wonder	if she can afford to.
Subj	Tense	Neg	Obj	Conj	Pred-2	Obj

(8) a.

She	went on an excessive diet	to slim down.
Subj	Pred-1	Mod

b.

She	does	not	look	healthy	and	I	am	afraid	that she should not have.
Subj	Tense	Neg	Pred-2	SC	Conj	Subj	Tense	Pred-2	Obj

(9) a.

She	also	had	eyelid surgery.
Subj	Mod	Pred-2	Obj

b.

She	is	suffering from	side effects	and	so	she	wishes	she had not.
Subj	Tense	Pred-2	Obj	Conj	Mod	Subj	Pred-2	Obj

(10) a.

She	got married	to a rich man	and	went on a honeymoon
Subj	Pred-2	Obj	Conj	Pred-2

to European countries.
Goal

b.

Her friends	envy	her	and	hope	they can,	too
Subj	Pred-2	Obj	Conj	Pred-2	Obj	Mod

when they get married.
Mod

(11) a.

She	gave birth to	two sons	and	hopes
Subj	Pred-2	Obj	Conj	Pred-2

to send them to a foreign country for their education.
Obj

b.

However,	her husband	is	worried	about money	and	does
Mod	Subj	Tense	Pred-2	Obj	Conj	Tense

not	want	to.
Neg	Pred-2	Obj

(12) a.

Furthermore,	her husband	is	worried
Mod	Subj	Tense	Pred-2

that if they go abroad they will experience culture shock.
Cause

b.

However,	she	is	not.
Mod	Subj	Tense	Neg

Special Tips on the Distance between the Two Predicate Phrases

• The Short Distance between the Two Predicate Phrases

✓ Subj + Tense + [Pred + (Obj) + (Mod)] + Subj + Tense + [Pred + (Obj) + (Mod)]
✓ Subj + Tense + [Pred + (Obj) + (Mod)] + Subj + Tense + [________________]

a. Jina has retired, but her husband has not retired yet.

b. Jina has retired, but her husband hasn't yet.

✓ Subj + Tense + [Pred + (Obj) + (Mod)] + Subj + Tense + [Pred + (Obj) + (Mod)]
✓ Subj + Tense + [Pred + (Obj) + (Mod)] + Subj + Tense + [________________]

a. Jimmy likes outdoor sports and his son likes outdoor sports too.

b. Jimmy likes outdoor sports and his son does, too.

✓ Subj + Tense + [Pred + (Obj) + (Mod)] + Subj + Tense + [Pred + (Obj) + (Mod)]
✓ Subj + Tense + [Pred + (Obj) + (Mod)] + Subj + Tense + [________________]

a. Jimmy works out every morning and his wife works out every morning, too.

b. Jimmy works out every morning and his wife does, too.

• The Long Distance between the Two Predicate Phrases

✓ Subj + Link + [Pred + Obj + Goal] + Subj + Link + [Pred + Obj + Goal]
✓ Subj + Link + [Pred + Obj + Goal] + Subj + Link + [________________]

a. Sue wants to send their two sons to a foreign country for their education. However, her husband is worried about money and does not want to send their two sons to a foreign country for their education.

b. Sue wants to send their two sons to a foreign country for their education. However, her husband is worried about money and does not want to.

✓ When two identical predicate phrases occur more than once, the second occurrence can be omitted. Ellipsis of the second predicate phrase is possible not only when the two predicate phrases are in the same sentence but also when the two predicate phrases are in two different sentences.

Dialogue 2

Chris : What do you think about that new guy, Tony?

Sue : He doesn't work out, and he is very fat.

Chris : I know. I told him to, but I am not sure if he will.

Sue : And it's not just his appearance that's the problem. He is a senior in high school, but he doesn't study hard.

Chris : I do not understand why he doesn't. I guess it's because he always plays video games excessively in the evening.

Sue : I know. His mom tells him not to, but I am not sure if he will listen to her.

Chris : Actually, he doesn't listen to anyone- not even his teachers. In fact, he often sends text messages to his friends, even during class.

Sue : Really?

Chris : Yeah! How do you think I found out so much about him? It's because he sends me text messages all the time.

Sue : Well, then you're as guilty as he is for reading messages in class.

Chris : Hey, but I get all A's.

Sue : Okay, I guess that excuses you.

Q. 위 대화문에서 술어와 수식어가 생략된 문장은?

① I told him to,

② I do not understand why he doesn't.

③ His mom tells him not to,

④ – not even his teachers.

정답 : ②

Exercise 1

다음 보기에 주어진 문장들의 상관관계를 잘 이해하고 이와 비슷한 패턴이 되도록 빈 칸에 적합한 단어나 표현을 쓰시오.

> **Ex** a. She is expected to sing a song at the party tonight, but I don't think she will sing a song at the party tonight.
>
> b. She is expected to sing a song at the party tonight, but I don't think she will.

(1) a. Sue has finished her homework, but her sister hasn't finished her homework yet.

b. Sue has finished her homework, but her sister (   ) (   ).

(2) a. John is fat and should exercise hard, but his pregnant wife should not exercise hard.

b. John is fat and should exercise hard, but his pregnant wife (   ) (   ).

(3) a. Brian is interested in studying abroad, and his brother is interested in studying abroad too.

b. Brian is interested in studying abroad, and his brother (   ) (   ).

Exercise 2

다음 보기에 주어진 문장들의 상관관계를 잘 이해하고 이와 비슷한 패턴이 되도록 빈 칸에 적합한 단어나 표현을 쓰시오.

Ex
a. The English teacher scolded the lazy student, but the math teacher didn't scold him.
b. The English teacher scolded the lazy student, but the math teacher didn't.
c. Judy often works out at a gym, and her friend Jinny works out at a gym too.
d. Judy often works out at a gym, and her friend Jinny does too.

(1) a. Soccer players don't like martial arts, and basketball players don't like martial arts, either.
b. Soccer players don't like martial arts, and basketball players (   ) (   ).

(2) a. Germany won 11 gold medals in 2012 London Olympics, and France won 11 gold medals at the 2012 London Olympics too.
b. Germany won 11 gold medals at the 2012 London Olympics, and France (   ) (   ).

Exercise 3

다음 보기에 주어진 두 문장의 상관관계를 잘 이해하고 이와 비슷한 패턴이 되도록 빈 칸에 적합한 단어나 표현을 쓰시오.

Ex

1. a. Did the athlete accept the umpire's decision?
   b. No, he didn't accept the umpire's decision.
   b'. No, he didn't.

2. a. Did the UK win 29 gold medals at the 2012 London Olympics?
   b. Yes, they won 29 gold medals at the 2012 London Olympics.
   b'. Yes, they did.

(1) a. Did you see him defeat his opponent at the match?
b. No, I didn't see him defeat his opponent at the match.
b'. No, I (   ).

(2) a. Do athletes respect umpires?
b. Yes, they respect them.
b'. Yes, they (   ).

(3) a. Are you proud of the Korean medalists?
b. Yes, I am proud of them.
b'. Yes, I (   ).

(4) a. Is he still dependent on his coach when making important decisions?
b. No, he is not dependent on his coach when making important decisions?
b'. No, he (   ).

Exercise 4

다음 보기에 주어진 문장의 패턴을 잘 관찰하고 물음에 답하시오.

Ex

1. a. Does your coach smoke?
   b. No, he doesn't.

2. a. Can he drive?
   b. Yes, he can.

3. a. Was the fencer upset?
   b. Yes, she was.

4. a. Have all the members of the national team come back?
   b. I am not sure, but I think they have.

5. a. Did she accept the umpire's decision?
   b. No, she didn't.

6. a. Did he appeal to the referee?
   b. Yes, he did.

7. a. Are you anxious to see them at the airport?
   b. Yes, I am.

8. a. Are they eligible to receive the award?
   b. Yes, they are.

1. 위 보기의 문장 중에서 문장 1b, 2b, 3b, 4b에서 생략된 단어들의 공통적인 문장성분은 무엇인가?

① 술어 ② 술어 + 수식어 ③ 술어 + 목적어 ④ 술어 + 직목 + 간목 + 수식어

2. 위 보기의 문장 중에서 문장 5b, 6b, 7b, 8b에서 생략된 단어들의 공통적인 문장성분은 무엇인가?

① 술어 ② 술어 + 수식어 ③ 술어 + 목적어 ④ 술어 + 직목 + 간목 + 수식어

3. 위 보기의 문장 중에서 문장 1b, 2b, 3b, 4b, 5b, 6b, 7b, 8b에서 생략된 단어들을 모두 아우를 수 있는 통합적인 개념은 무엇인가?

① 술어 ② 술어 + 수식어 ③ 술어 + 목적어 ④ 술어구(predicate phrase)

Wrap Up

1. 술어의 생략

(1) a. Subj + Tense + Pred-1

b. Subj + Tense + ______

Ex 1 a. Sylvia has retired, but her husband hasn't retired yet.

b. Sylvia has retired, but her husband hasn't yet.

2. 술어와 수식어의 생략

(2) a. Subj + Tense + Pred-1 + Mod

b. Subj + Tense + ______

Ex 2 a. She works out regularly, but her husband doesn't work out regularly.

b. She works out regularly, but her husband doesn't .

3. 술어와 목적어의 생략

(3) a. Subj + Tense + Pred-2 + Obj

b. Subj + Tense + ______

Ex 3 a. She is starting a new business although her husband wants her not to start a new business.

b. She is starting a new business although her husband wants her not to.

4. 술어, 목적어, 장소의 생략

(4) a. Subj + Tense + Pred-3 + Obj + Loc

b. Subj + Tense + ______________

Ex 4 a. She located her office in downtown Seoul though she was advised not to locate her office downtown Seoul.

b. She located her office in downtown Seoul though she was advised not to.

5. 술어, 목적지, 수식어의 생략

(5) a. Subj + Tense + Pred-2 + Goal + Mod

b. Subj + Tense + ______________

Ex 5 a. Jinny wants to go to UCLA for a language program.

b. Her parents are not well off and wonder if she can afford to.

6. 술어, 목적어 그리고 소재의 생략

(6) a. Subj + Tense + Pred-3 + Obj + Substance

b. Subj + Tense + ______________

Ex 6 a. She furnished her office with luxurious furniture though she was advised not to furnish her office with luxurious furniture.

b. She furnished her office with luxurious furniture though she was advised not to.

7. 술어와 직목, 간목, 수식어의 생략

(7) a. Subj + Tense + Pred-3 + DO + IO + Mod

b. Subj + Tense + ____________________

Ex 7 a. She gave birth to two sons and hopes to send the two sons to a foreign country for their education.

b. However, her husband worries about money and does not want to.

Memo

UNIT 14 시제는 어디로 갔을까?

Where is Tense?

Warm Up

본 단원에서는 의문문의 형성과정에 대해서 학습하도록 하겠습니다. 의문문은 Yes/No로 대답할 수 있는 Yes-No Question과 Yes/No로 대답할 수 없고 구체적인 정보를 주어야 하는 WH-Question으로 분류할 수 있습니다. Yes-No Question은 다시 주절이 Yes-No Question인 경우와 종속절이 Yes-No Question은 경우로 분류할 수 있습니다. WH-Question도 주절이 WH-Question인 경우와 종속절이 WH-Question인 경우로 나눌 수 있습니다. 주절이 의문문인 경우는 직접의문문이 되고 종속절이 의문문인 경우는 간접의문문이 됩니다.

1. Yes-No Question

● 주절의 Yes-No Question

· **Comp**(+Q) + Subj + **Tense** + Pred

● 종속절의 Yes-No Question

· Comp + Subj + Tense + Pred + **Comp**(+Q) + Subject + Tense + Pred

if, whether

2. WH-Question

- 주절의 WH-Question

· **Comp**(+Q) + Subj + **Tense** + Pred + **WH-element**

· **Comp**(+Q) + Subj + **Tense** + Pred + Comp + Subj + Tense + Pred + **WH-element**

- 종속절에서의 WH-Question

· Comp + Subj + Tense + Pred + **Comp**(+Q) + Subj + Tense + Pred + **WH-element**

Qviz

다음 보기에 주어진 문장을 살펴보고 물음에 답하시오.

Ex

1. a. John is not **tall**.
   b. **Is** he short?

2. a. Judy **does** not **like** him.
   b. **Does** she like tall guys?

3. a. She **hasn't met any** short guys.
   b. **Has** she already **met** some tall guys?

4. a. She **will** not even **go on a date** with a guy of average height.
   b. **Will** she **go on a date** with a guy of exceptional height?

1. 위 보기에 주어진 문장은 평서문과 의문문으로 구성되어 있으며 평서문에서 시제와 술어가 분리되어 있다. 평서문에서 의문문을 형성하기 위해서 공통적으로 일어나는 현상은 무엇인가?

① Predicate을 Comp로 이동시킨다.
② Neg를 Comp로 이동시킨다.
③ Tense를 Comp로 이동시킨다.
④ Aspect를 Comp로 이동시킨다.

Ex

1. a. John **likes** attractive ladies.
   b. John **does** not **like** unattractive ladies.
   c. **Does** he often **talk** to the attractive ladies?
   d. John **does like** attractive ladies.

2. a. He **met** the attractive ladies the day before yesterday.
   b. He **did** not **meet** the unattractive ladies the day before yesterday.
   c. **Did** he **meet** them today?
   d. He **did meet** the attractive ladies the day before yesterday.

3. a. He **succeeded** in winning one attractive lady's favor.
   b. He **did** not **succeed** in winning her parents' favor.
   c. **Did** he **succeed** in winning her parents' favor?
   d. He **did succeed** in winning one attractive lady's favor.

2. 위 보기에 주어진 문장은 긍정평서문(1a, 2a, 3a), 부정문(1b, 2b, 3b), 그리고 의문문(1c, 2c, 3c)로 구성되어 있다. 긍정평서문에서는 시제와 술어가 하나로 융합되어 있으며(1a, 2a, 3a), 부정문(1b, 2b, 3b)과 의문문(1c, 2c, 3c)에서는 시제와 술어가 분리되어있다. 긍정평서문에서도 원래 시제와 술어가 분리되어 있다고 간주하면(1d, 2d, 3d) 어떤 점에서 더 장점이 있나?(둘을 고르시오)

① 부정문을 쉽게 만들 수 있다. ② 의문문을 더 쉽게 만들 수 있다.
③ 조건문을 더 쉽게 만들 수 있다. ④ 감탄문을 더 쉽게 만들 수 있다.

3. 보기의 문장 1d에서 1a가 도출되고 문장 2d에서 2a가 도출되며, 문장 3d에서 문장 3a가 도출되는 과정을 가장 잘 나타내는 표현은?

① Tense와 Predicate의 융합 ② Tense와 Predicate의 분리
③ Aspect와 Predicate의 분리 ④ Aspect와 Predicate의 융합

Lecture 1

Yes-No Question

- 주절의 Yes-No Question

Comp(+Q) + Subj + **Tense** + Pred

· Tense ➡ Comp

Ex 1. a. John **will** not go fishing at the river.

b. **Will** he go swimming at the river?

2. a. Sue **goes** on diets to lose weight.

b. **Does** her sister go on diets to lose weight too?

- 종속절의 Yes-No Question

Comp + Subj + Tense + Pred + **Comp**(+Q) + Subj + Tense + Pred

· if, whether ➡ Comp

Ex 1. Tony: **Does** your brother intend to immigrate to Canada next year?

James: I do not know **if** he will immigrate to Canada next year or not.

2. Jina: **Does** your sister come back to Korea next year?

Bill: It is not certain **whether** she will come back to Korea next year or not.

Sentence Analysis

(1) a. The CEO of a cosmetics business has two daughters. The first daughter is a beauty while the second daughter is not. They are interested in the cosmetics business.

b. **Will** the CEO hand down the business to the first daughter or the second daughter?

(2) a. The first daughter thinks that she should inherit the business because she is the first daughter. The second daughter thinks that she is equally qualified to inherit the business.

b. The CEO does not know **whether** she should hand down her business to the first daughter or the second daughter.

(3) a. The CEO is in a dilemma. The CEO says that she will hand down the business to whoever goes to a prestigious university.

b. **Did** the two daughters both study hard to go to a prestigious university?

(4) a. The second daughter studied hard to pass the entrance exam. The first daughter thought she didn't have to study hard because she was a beauty.

b. **Did** the second daughter get in to a prestigious university?

(5) a. The first daughter says that her sister is not qualified to run the business even though she went to a prestigious university.

b. It is not certain **if** the CEO will hand down the business to her second daughter.

(6) a. The first daughter says that she should inherit the business because she is a beauty. The second daughter says that she should inherit the business because she goes to a prestigious university.

b. It is not **obvious** whether the CEO will keep her promise or not.

(7) a. On the one hand, the CEO should hand down her business to her first daughter because she is a beauty. On the other hand, the CEO should hand down her business to her second daughter because she goes to a prestigious university.

b. The husband of the CEO asked **if** she would hand down the business at all.

(8) a. The CEO came up with another idea. The CEO says that she will hand down the business to whoever wins the beauty contest. The CEO thinks that her second daughter will give up because she is not a beauty.

b. **Will** the two daughters both participate in the beauty contest?

(9) a. It is obvious that the first daughter will take part in the beauty contest.

b. It is not obvious **if** the second daughter will take part in the beauty contest or not.

(10) a. The husband of the CEO wants the second daughter to inherit the business.

b. The CEO doesn't know **whether or not** he will give advice to the second daughter.

Special Tips on Yes-No Questions

Types of Questions

- Yes-No Questions

· Main Clause Yes-No Questions

Comp(+Q) + Subj + **Tense** + Pred

(Ex)

1. a. The first daughter is gorgeous.
   b. **Is** the second daughter gorgeous as well?
2. a. The first daughter wants to inherit the business.
   b. Does the second daughter want to inherit the business?

· Embedded Yes-No Questions

Comp + Subj + Tense + Pred (Main Clause) + **Comp**(+Q) + Subj + Tense + Pred (Embedded Clause)

Comp(+Q) ← if, whether

(Ex)

1. a. The second daughter went to a prestigious university.
   b. However, the CEO still wonders (Main Clause)
   if she should hand down the business to her. (Embedded Clause)
2. a. The second daughter went to a prestigious university.
   b. However, it is not obvious (Main Clause)
   whether or not she will inherit the business. (Embedded Clause)

Dialogue 1

Sarah: I'm really upset. My best friend's husband is divorcing her!

Tom: Oh my goodness! Didn't he love his wife?

Sarah: No, he didn't love his wife. He's actually a pretty bad husband.

Tom: Really?

Sarah: Yes, he complains a lot and criticizes everything she does.

Tom: If he didn't love his wife, then didn't she want a divorce anyway?!

Sarah: No, she didn't want a divorce. She was hoping they could see a marriage counselor and solve their problems together. She's also worried about money.

Tom: Has she applied for the job at the art gallery?

Sarah: Yes, she has applied for the job at the art gallery. I hope she is successful. She will need the money after the divorce.

Q. 위 대화문에서 어떠한 방법으로 Yes-No Question이 형성되나?

① Tense를 Comp로 이동 ② Predicate을 Comp로 이동

③ Link를 Comp로 이동 ④ Aspect를 Comp로 이동

정답 : ①

Exercise 1

1. 다음 보기의 주어진 두 문장의 상관관계를 잘 분석하고 이와 유사한 패턴이 되도록 빈칸에 적절한 단어를 입력하세요.

> Ex
> a. She **is** running a cosmetics business.
> b. **Is** she running a cosmetics business?

(1) a. She is a beauty.

b. (   ) she a beauty?

(2) a. They are both interested in the cosmetics business.

b. (   ) they both interested in the cosmetics business?

(3) a. The CEO will hand down the business to her first daughter.

b. (   ) the CEO hand down the business to her first daughter?

(4) a. The second daughter went to a prestigious university.

b. (   ) the second daughter go to a prestigious university?

Exercise 2

1. 다음 보기의 주어진 두 문장의 상관관계를 잘 분석하고 이와 유사한 패턴이 되도록 빈칸에 적절한 단어를 입력하세요.

> Ex
> a. The second daughter **did not** take part in the beauty contest.
> b. **Didn't** the second daughter take part in the beauty contest?

(1) a. The second daughter is not a beauty.
b. (   ) the second daughter a beauty?

(2) a. The first daughter does not have to study hard.
b. (   ) the first daughter have to study hard?

(3) a. The parents do not know who they should hand down the business to.
b. (   ) the parents know who they should hand down the business to?

(4) a. She will not hand down the business to whoever wins the beauty contest.
b. (   ) she hand down the business to whoever wins the beauty contest?

Exercise 3

1. 다음 보기의 주어진 두 문장의 상관관계를 잘 분석하고 이와 유사한 패턴이 되도록 빈칸에 알맞은 문장을 입력하세요.

> **Ex**
> a. She does not know.
> b. Can he drive a car?
> c. She does not know if he can drive a car or not.

(1) a. It is not certain.

b. Will she hand down the business to her first daughter?

c. It is not certain (　　　　　　) (　　　　　　) (　　　　　　) hand down the business to her first daughter or not.

(2) a. People are anxious to know.

b. Did she go to a prestigious university?

c. People are anxious to know (　　　　　　) (　　　　　　) (　　　　　　) to a prestigious university or not.

Ex a. The husband of the CEO is not sure.

b. Will the CEO hand down the business?

c. The husband of the CEO is not sure whether or not the CEO will hand down the business.

(3) a. It is not obvious.

b. Will she keep her promise?

c. It is not obvious (　　　　　　) (　　　　　　) (　　　　　　) (　　　　　　) (　　　　　　) keep her promise.

(4) a. The CEO does not know.

b. Will he give advice to the second daughter?

c. The CEO does not know (　　　　　　) (　　　　　　) (　　　　　　) (　　　　　　) (　　　　　　) give advice to the second daughter.

(5) a. People are anxious to know.

b. Did she go to a prestigious university?

c. People are anxious to know (　　　　　　) (　　　　　　) (　　　　　　) (　　　　　　) (　　　　　　) to a prestigious university.

Lecture 2

WH-Question

- 주절의 WH-Question

Comp(+Q) + Subject + **Tense** + Predicate + **WH-element**

· Tense ➡ Comp, WH-element ➡ Comp

Ex

1) Waiter: Are you ready to order, ma'am?

Maria: **What do** you recommend?

2) Julia: He is out to lunch.

Maria: **When do** you expect him back?

- 종속절의 WH-Question

Comp + Subject + Tense + Predicate + **Comp**(+Q) + Subject + Tense + Predicate + **WH-element**

· WH-element ➡ Comp

Ex

1) Brian: Did your son go out on a date?

Kerry: Yes, but I do not know **who** he is on a date with.

2) Sue: Is you daughter seeing anyone these days?

Jenny: Yes, but I do not know **who** she will marry.

Sentence Analysis

(1) a. The first daughter is gorgeous. The second daughter is rather homely.

b. **What plastic surgery will** the second daughter have to improve her looks?

(2) a. She has fine wrinkles around her eyes.

b. **Which hospital will** she go to for a facelift?

(3) a. She does not have a sharp nose.

b. **Which plastic surgeon will** she consult about sharpening her nose?

(4) a. She does not have double eyelids.

b. **Which nurse will** she talk to about making an appointment with the doctor?

(5) a. She is near-sighted and wears glasses.

b. **What kind of optical operation will** she have to wash her hands of glasses?

(6) a. She has an irregular set of teeth.

b. Her sister does not know **which dental clinic** she will visit to straighten her teeth.

(7) a. She has a square jaw line. She has not had surgery to revise her square jaw yet because of the high cost of the operation. She will ask her dad for help.

b. He doesn't know **how much** it will cost to have the operation.

(8) a. She wanted her lips to be a bit fuller. She had an operation on her lips.

b. Her family does not know **at which hospital** she had the operation.

(9) a. After the surgery, she had double eyelids, a prominent nose, and full lips. The first daughter and the second daughter both participated in the beauty contest.
b. Now it is hard to predict **which daughter** will win the beauty contest.

(10) a. The mom wanted her first daughter to win the beauty contest.
b. It is still not decided **which daughter** the CEO will hand down her business to.

(11) a. The dad wanted his second daughter to win the beauty contest.
b. **Who does** he think his wife will hand down the business to?

(12) a. It turned out that the second daughter got higher marks than the first daughter in the beauty contest.
b. The employees do not know yet **who** will be the next CEO of the cosmetics business.

(13) a. The mom is not satisfied with the outcome. The dad is happy with the outcome.
b. The employees cannot wait to see **how** the next CEO will run the business.

(14) a. At the inauguration ceremony the new CEO asked a question of the employees.
b. She asked them **which person** God would help. They answered that God helps those who help themselves.

Special Tips on WH-Questions

Types of WH-Questions

- Main Clause WH-Questions

Comp(+Q) + Subj + **Tense** + Pred + **WH-element**

Ex 1. a. She does not have a sharp nose.
b. **Which doctor will** she consult about having an operation?

Comp(+Q) + Subj + **Tense** + Pred + Comp(+Q) + Subj + Tense + Pred + **WH-element**

Main Clause — Embedded Clause

Ex 2. a. The CEO has not made a decision yet.
b. Who do you think she will hand down the business to?

Main Clause: Who do you think — Embedded Clause: she will hand down the business to?

In main clause wh-questions, tense and wh-elements both move to the comp position to make direct wh-questions. For example, in simple sentences such as (1b) 'will' and 'which doctor' move to the comp position to create direct a wh-question. In complex sentences such as (2b), the main clause tense verb 'do' and the embedded clause wh-element 'who' both move to the main clause comp position to make a direct wh-question.

- Embedded Clause WH-Questions

Comp + Subj + Tense + Pred + **Comp**(+Q) + Subj + Tense + Pred + **WH-element**

Main Clause — Embedded Clause

Ex 1. a. The CEO hasn't made a decision yet.

b. Her husband doesn't know (Main Clause)

who she will hand down the business to. (Embedded Clause)

Comp + Subj + Tense + Pred + **Comp**(+Q) + Subj + Tense + Pred + **WH-element**

Main Clause — Embedded Clause

Ex 2. a. The CEO hasn't made a decision yet.

b. Does her husband know (Main Clause)

who she will hand down the business to? (Embedded Clause)

In embedded clause wh-questions, only the embedded clause wh-elements move to the comp position to make indirect wh-questions. For example, in complex sentences such as (1b), only the embedded clause wh-element 'who' moves to the comp position to create an indirect wh-question. The same is true of sentence (2b), where only the embedded clause wh-element 'who' moves to the comp position.

Dialogue 2

Jack: Oh! Who is Tony kissing?

Mary: Tony is kissing his new girlfriend.

Jack: Really? What happened to his last girlfriend?

Mary: Well, it's a long story. She dumped him after he was late to her birthday party.

Jack: Are you serious? That doesn't seem like such a big mistake!

Mary: Well, he forgot to set his alarm clock. That wasn't the only mistake he made. Her mom got really sick after the birthday party.

Jack: Why was he blamed for that?

Mary: He made a chocolate birthday cake. Her mom ate some cake and became really sick. Tony had used bad milk and rotten eggs accidentally. He was blamed for that mistake.

Jack: Well, he seems to be a better kisser than a chef then! Haha!

Q. 위 대화문에서 어떠한 방법으로 WH-Question이 형성되나?(둘을 고르시오)

① Tense를 Comp로 이동　　② Predicate을 Comp로 이동

③ 의문사를 Comp로 이동　　④ Link를 Comp로 이동

정답 : ①, ③

Exercise 1

1. 다음 보기의 주어진 두 문장의 상관관계를 잘 분석하고 이와 유사한 패턴이 되도록 빈칸에 적절한 단어를 입력하세요.

> Ex
>
> a. She ***was*** talking to ***a tall*** **man.** ➡
>
> b. **Which man was** she talking to?

(1) a. She ***will*** go to ***a*** **hospital** for a facelift.

b. (   ) (   ) (   ) she go to for a facelift?

(2) a. She ***will*** consult ***a*** **plastic surgeon** to make her nose pointier.

b. (   ) (   ) (   ) (   ) she consult to make her nose pointier?

(3) a. The CEO ***will*** hand down the business to ***her second*** **daughter.**

b. (   ) (   ) (   ) the CEO hand down the business to?

(4) a. She ***will*** talk to ***a*** **nurse** for an appointment with a doctor.

b. (   ) (   ) (   ) she talk to make an appointment with a doctor?

Exercise 2

1. 다음 보기의 주어진 두 문장의 상관관계를 잘 분석하고 이와 유사한 패턴이 되도록 빈칸에 적절한 단어를 입력하세요.

> Ex a. He talked to ***a tall woman***. ➡
>
> b. **Who did** he talk to?

(1) a. She handed down the business to ***one of her daughters***.

b. (   ) (   ) she hand down the business to.

(2) a. She had ***the operation*** to improve her looks.

b. (   ) (   ) she have ***done*** to improve her looks?

(3) a. The plastic surgery cost her ***a lot***.

b. (   ) (   ) (   ) the plastic surgery cost her?

(4) a. She wants to alter her square jaw ***in a nearby hospital***.

b. (   ) (   ) (   ) want to alter her ***square jaw***?

Exercise 3

1. 다음 보기의 주어진 두 문장의 상관관계를 잘 분석하고 이와 유사한 패턴이 되도록 빈칸에 적절한 단어를 입력하세요

> Ex
> a. Sue does not know.
> b. **Who should** she consult?
> c. Sue does not know **who** she should consult.

(1) a. The second daughter is wondering.
b. What plastic surgery will she have?
c. The second daughter is wondering (　　　　) (　　　　) (　　　　) (　　　　) will have.

(2) a. Her sister does not know.
b. Which dental clinic will she visit to straighten her teeth?
c. Her sister does not know (　　　　) (　　　　) (　　　　) (　　　　) will visit to straighten her teeth.

(3) a. Her family does not know.
b. Where did she have the operation?
c. Her family does not know (　　　　) (　　　　) (　　　　) the operation?

(4) a. The employees cannot wait to see.
b. How will the next CEO run the business?
c. The employees cannot wait to see (　　　　) the next CEO (　　　　) run the business.

Exercise 4

1. 다음 보기의 주어진 두 문장의 상관관계를 잘 분석하고 이와 유사한 패턴이 되도록 빈칸에 적절한 단어를 입력하세요.

> **Ex**
> a. Does he think?
> b. Who will she hand down her business to?
> c. Who does he think she will hand down her business to?

(1) a. Does the second daughter think?

b. Who will God help?

c. (   ) (   ) the second daughter think God will help?

(2) a. Does the dad want?

b. Which daughter will inherit the business?

c. (   ) (   ) (   ) the dad want to inherit the business?

Exercise 5

1. 다음 보기의 주어진 두 문장의 상관관계를 잘 분석하고 이와 유사한 패턴이 되도록 빈칸에 적절한 단어를 입력하세요.

Ex

a. Do they know?

b. How will she run the business?

c. Do they know how she will run the business?

(1) a. Does her family know?

b. Where did she have the operation?

c. (   ) her family know (   ) she had the operation?

(2) a. Do the employees wonder?

b. How will the next CEO run the business?

c. (   ) the employees wonder (   ) the next CEO will run the business?

Wrap Up

1. Yes-No Question

- 주절의 Yes-No Question

Comp(+**Q**) + Subj + **Tense** + Predicate

> 1. **Will** the CEO hand down the business to the first daughter or second daughter?
> 2. **Did** the two daughters both study hard to go to a prestigious university?

- 종속절의 Yes-No Question

Comp + Subj + Tense + Pred (Main Clause) + **Comp**(+**Q**) + Subj + Tense + Pred (Embedded Clause)

if, whether

> 1. It is not certain (Main Clause)
>
>   **if** the CEO will hand down the business to her second daughter. (Embedded Clause)
>
> 2. The CEO does not know (Main Clause) **whether** she should hand down her business to the first daughter or second daughter. (Embedded Clause)

2. WH-Question

● 주절의 WH-Question

· **Comp**(+Q) + Subj + **Tense** + Pred + **WH-element**

> Ex **What plastic surgery will** the second daughter have to improve her looks?

· **Comp**(+Q) + Subj + **Tense** + Pred + Comp(+Q) + Subj + Tense + Pred + **WH-element**

Main Clause / Embedded Clause

> Ex **Who does** he think (Main Clause) his wife will hand down the business to? (Embedded Clause)

● 종속절에서의 WH-Question

· Comp + Subj + Tense + Pred + **Comp**(+Q) + Subj + Tense + Pred + **WH-element**

Main Clause / Embedded Clause

> Ex 1. Her family doesn't know (Main Clause) **at which hospital** she had the operation. (Embedded Clause)
>
> 2. The employees can't wait to see (Main Clause) **how** the next CEO will run the business. (Embedded Clause)

GRAMMAR DNA 총정리 연습문제

UNIT 9~14

PART 1. 주어진 문장의 종속절을 시제절에서 비시제절로 변화시키시오.

1. a. John regrets that he has spent all of his inheritance.
   b. John regrets (   ) (   ) all of his inheritance.

2. a. After he had lost all his money, he began to miss his parents.
   b. (   ) (   ) (   ) all his money, he began to miss his parents.

3. a. The child began to cry when he was scolded.
   b. The child began to cry (   ) (   ) (   ).

4. a. Sue believes that her daughter is a good student.
   b. Sue believes (   ) (   ) (   ) (   ) a good student.

5. a. Because she did not have money, she could not afford to buy a car.
   b. (   ) (   ) (   ), she could not afford to buy a car.

PART 2. 아래 보기의 예문은 종속절이 시제절에서 비시제로 변화되는 과정을 보여주고 있다. 예문을 잘 살펴보고 물음에 답하시오.

Ex

1. a. You should be careful (주절(시제절)) **when you deal with poisonous animals** (종속절(시제절)).

   b. You should be careful (주절(시제절)) **when dealing with poisonous animals** (종속절(비시제절)).

2. c. Sue saw (주절(시제절)) **her son was smoking a cigarette in the living room** (종속절(시제절)).

   d. Sue saw (주절(시제절)) **her son smoking a cigarette in the living room** (종속절(비시제절)).

3. e. **While I was running for a bus,** (종속절(시제절)) I tripped over a stone (주절(시제절)).

   f. **While running for a bus,** (종속절(비시제절)) I tripped over a stone (주절(시제절)).

4. g. John remembers (주절(시제절)) **that he had mailed the letter to his boss** (종속절(시제절)).

   h. John remembers (주절(시제절)) **having mailed the letter to his boss** (종속절(비시제절)).

6. 비시제절인 종속절이 현재분사를 사용하는 문장 3개를 고르시오.

① 1b ② 2d ③ 3f ④ 4h

7. 비시제절인 종속절이 진행의 의미를 가지고 있는 문장 2개를 고르시오.

① 1b ② 2d ③ 3f ④ 4h

8. 비시제절인 종속절이 동명사를 사용하는 문장 1개를 고르시오.

① 1b ② 2d ③ 3f ④ 4h

9. 비시제절인 종속절에서 현재분사를 사용하는 경우의 특징을 가장 잘 나타낸 문장은?

① 진행의 의미가 있거나 또는 부사절이다.

② 완료를 나타낸다.

③ 문장에서 목적어 역할을 한다.

④ 문장에서 수식어 역할을 한다.

10. 종속절이 시제절에서 비시제절로 전환될 때 문장 4h의 remember와 같은 패턴을 보이는 동사 2개를 고르시오.

① admit ② expect ③ think ④ deny

PART 3. 아래 보기의 예문을 잘 살펴보고 물음에 답하시오.

Ex

1. a. Students are bothering their professors.
   b. Professors are being bothered by their students.

2. c. He pushed the button.
   d. The button was pushed by him.

3. e. Sue has completed a new project.
   f. A new project has been completed by Sue.

4. g. Joshua is a genius.
   h. He will be an aerospace engineer.

5. i. She has already finished the work.
   j. How speedy she is!

11. 위 보기의 예문 중에서 언더라인된 단어는 다양한 기능을 하고 있다. 언더라인된 단어가 진행(progressive aspect)을 나타내는 문장은?

① 1b ② 2d ③ 3f ④ 4h ⑤ 5j

12. 언더라인된 단어가 완료(perfective aspect)를 나타내는 문장을 고르시오.

① 1b ② 2d ③ 3f ④ 4h ⑤ 5j

13. 언더라인된 단어가 시제(Tense)를 나타내는 문장을 고르시오.

① 1b ② 2d ③ 3f ④ 4h ⑤ 5j

14. 언더라인된 단어가 술어(Predicate)인 문장을 고르시오.

① 1b ② 2d ③ 3f ④ 4h ⑤ 5j

15. 언더라인된 단어가 보문어(Comp)인 문장을 고르시오.

① 1b ② 2d ③ 3f ④ 4h ⑤ 5j

PART 4. 아래 보기의 예문을 잘 살펴보고 물음에 답하시오.

Ex

1. a. Bill does not like people touching his baby.
   b. Bill does not like his baby being touched by people.

2. c. Maria does not expect her parents to treat her like a child.
   d. Maria does not expect to be treated like a child by her parents.

3. e. Sue resents that her husband has forgotten her birthday.
   f. Sue resents her husband having forgotten her birthday.

4. g. Jina hoped that she would finish the work on time, but it was not successful.
   h. Jina hoped to have finished the work on time.

5. i. When he was given something to eat, he stopped crying.
   j. When (being) given something to eat, he stopped crying.

16. 문장 1b의 'being'의 역할은 무엇인가?

① Tense
② Aspect
③ like와 touched를 연결하는 Link
④ his baby와 touched를 연결하는 Link
⑤ Predicate

17. 문장 2d의 'to be'의 역할은 무엇인가?

① Tense
② Aspect
③ not와 treated를 연결하는 Link
④ expected와 treated를 연결하는 Link
⑤ Predicate

18. 문장 3f의 having의 역할은 무엇인가?

① Tense
② Aspect
③ her husband와 forgotten을 연결하는 Link
④ resents와 forgotten을 연결하는 Link
⑤ Predicate

19. 문장 4h의 to have의 역할은 무엇인가?

① Tense
② Aspect
③ hoped와 finished를 연결하는 Link
④ hoped와 the work를 연결하는 Link
⑤ Predicate

20. 문장 5j의 being의 역할은 무엇인가?

① 진행
② 완료
③ 주절과 종속절을 연결하는 optional Link
④ when과 given을 연결하는 Link
⑤ 시제

PART 5. 아래 보기의 예문을 잘 살펴보고 물음에 답하시오.

Ex

A형

1\. a. It is possible (주절) that **John** will break up with his girlfriend. (종속절)

b. *__John__ is possible (주절) to break up with his girlfriend. (종속절) (* = 비문법적이 문장)

B형

2\. c. It seems (주절) that **John** has insomnia. (종속절)

d. **John** seems (주절) to have insomnia. (종속절)

3\. e. It seems (주절) that **John** was a rich man. (종속절)

f. **John** seems (주절) to have been a rich man. (종속절)

위 보기에 주어진 예문을 보면 종속절의 주어가 주절 주어로 이동할 수 없는 A형 술어(1b의 impossible)도 있고 이동할 수 있는 B형 술어(2d, 3f의 seems)도 있다. 다음 주어진 술어의 유형을 명시하시오.

21.

appear, unlikely, likely, said(수동형)

① A형 ② B형

22.

easy, difficult, surprising, interesting

① A형 ② B형

23.

prove, turn out, certain, expected(수동형)

① A형　　② B형

24.

probable, hard, impossible, boring

① A형　　② B형

25. 문장 3f의 종속절에서 "to be"를 사용하지 않고 "to have been"을 사용하는 이유는 무엇인가?

① 주절과 종속절의 시제가 다르기 때문

② 주절과 종속절의 시제가 같기 때문

③ 주절의 동사가 1가 술어이기 때문

④ 종속절의 동사가 2가 술어이기 때문

PART 6. 주어진 두 문장이 같은 의미의 문장이 되기 위해서 빈칸에 들어갈 적절한 단어를 넣으시오.

26. a. That the world is witnessing a power shift from the West to Asia worries a superpower.

b. ( ) ( ) a superpower that the world is witnessing a power shift from the West to Asia.

27. a. To attend the speech through a random selection process was not easy.

b. ( ) ( ) ( ) easy to attend the speech through a random selection process.

28. a. Does how the White House selected HUFS really matter?

b. ( ) ( ) really matter how the White House selected HUFS?

29. a. The time to unify North and South Korea has come.

b. The time has come ( ) ( ) North and South Korea.

30. a. The judges did not make why the athlete was disqualified clearly understood.

b. The judges did not make ( ) ( ) ( ) why the athlete was disqualified.

PART 7. 주어진 두 문장이 같은 의미의 문장이 되기 위해서 빈칸에 들어갈 적절한 단어를 넣으시오.

31. a. Sue has finished her homework, but her sister has not finished her homework yet.

b. Sue has finished her homework, but her sister ( ) ( ) yet.

32. a. John is fat and should exercise hard, but his pregnant wife should not exercise hard.

b. John is fat and should exercise hard, but his pregnant wife ( ) ( ).

33. a. Brian is interested in studying abroad, and his brother is interested in studying abroad too.

b. Brian is interested in studying abroad, and his brother ( ) ( ).

34. a. Soccer players don't like martial arts and basket players don't like martial arts either.

b. Soccer players don't like martial arts and basketball players ( ) ( ).

35. a. Germany won gold medals at the 2012 London Olympics, and France won gold medals at the 2012 London Olympics too.

b. Germany won gold medals at the 2012 London Olympics, and France (　　　　　) (　　　　　).

PART 8. 아래 보기의 예문을 잘 살펴보고 물음에 답하시오.

Ex

1. a. The CEO will hand down the business to the second daughter.
   b. The first daughter didn't get in to a prestigious university.

2. c. It is not obvious (　　　　) or not the CEO will keep her promise.
   d. The husband of the CEO asked (　　　　) she would hand down the business at all.

3. e. How much will it cost to have the operation?
   f. He doesn't know (　　　　) (　　　　) (　　　　) (　　　　) cost to have the operation.

36. 문장 1a가 직접의문문이 되기 위해서 Comp자리로 이동해야 하는 단어는?

① The CEO　② will　③ hand down　④ the business

37. 문장 1b가 직접의문문이 되기 위해서 Comp자리로 이동해야 하는 단어는?

① The first daughter　② didn't　③ get　④ a prestigious university

38. 문장 2c의 종속절을 간접의문으로 만들기 위해서 종속절의 Comp자리에 들어가야 할 단어는?

① whether　② if　③ will　④ keep

39. 문장 2d의 종속절을 간접의문으로 만들기 위해서 종속절의 Comp자리에 들어가야 할 단어는?

① would ② if ③ did ④ hand down

40. 문장 3f의 종속절을 간접의문으로 만들기 위해서 종속절의 빈칸에 들어가야 할 단어는?

____.

Memo

정답

UNIT 1

Warm Up

QUIZ 1

1. ①
2. ④

QUIZ 2

1. 보라색 동사는 시제동사와 술어동사를 연결해 주는 역할을 한다.

QUIZ 3

1. ②
2. ③

Lecture 1

Exercise 1

1. ① Subject, ② Tense, ③ Neg, ④ Link, ⑤ Aspect
2. (1) ⑤
   (2) ④
   (3) ②
   (4) ③
3. ②
4. ③
5. (1) Subject
   (2) Tense
   (3) Predicate
   (4) Neg
   (5) Predicate
   (6) Link
   (7) Aspect
   (8) Modifier
6. (1) ①
   (2) ①
   (3) ②
   (4) ①
   (5) ③

Lecture 2

Exercise 1

1. ③
2. ①
3. ④
4. ①
5. (1) Subject
   (2) Comp
   (3) Tense
   (4) Aspect
   (5) Neg
   (6) Link
   (7) Tense
   (8) Comp
6. 빈도분사는 Neg와 Link 사이에 위치한다.

UNIT 2

Warm Up

QUIZ 1

1. ③
2. ①

QUIZ 2

1. ④
2. ②

QUIZ 3

1. ③
2. ③

Lecture 1

Exercise 1

1. ① Subject, ② Tense, ③ Neg, ④ Predicate-1
2. ①
3. ④
4. (1) ③
   (2) ④
   (3) ①
   (4) ⑤
5. (1) Subject
   (2) Tense
   (3) Neg
   (4) Predicate-1
   (5) Predicate-1
   (6) Modifier
6. (1) ④
   (2) ③
   (3) ④

Lecture 2

Exercise 1

1. ①
2. ①
3. ②
4. ①

Exercise 2

1. (1) Expletive
   (2) Predicate-1
   (3) Tense
   (4) Proposition
   (5) Comp
2. (1) appears, to, have, slightly
   (2) to, be, defeated
   (3) to, be
   (4) to, see
   (5) to, have, been
   (6) to, have, passed

UNIT 3

Warm Up

QUIZ 1

1. ②
2. ①
3. ②
4. ③
5. ④
6. ②
7. ③
8. ④

Lecture 1

Exercise 1

1. ②
2. ①, ②, ③
3. ①
4. ②

5. ③

Exercise 2

1. (1) Tense
   (2) Predicate-2
   (3) Subject Complement

Exercise 3

1. (1) Neg
   (2) Object
   (3) Comp

Exercise 4

1. (1) Predicate-2
   (2) Location
   (3) Comp

Exercise 5

1. ④
2. ②
3. ④
4. ①
5. ④
6. ① c
   ② b
   ③ a

Lecture 2

Exercise 1

1. ①, ②, ③, ④
2. ①
3. ②
4. ③
5. ④

Exercise 2

1. ① Predicate-2
   ② Goal
   ③ Source

Exercise 3

1. ① Tense
   ② Predicate-2
   ③ Substance

Exercise 4

1. Cause

Exercise 5

1. ③
2. (1) ②
   (2) ③
   (3) ④
   (4) ④
   (5) ①
   (6) ③
   (7) ②

UNIT 4

Warm Up

QUIZ 1

1. ③
2. ①
3. ②
4. ③
5. ④
6. ②
7. ③
8. ④

Lecture 1

Exercise 1

1. (1) ③

(2) ②

(3) ③

(4) ②

2. ②

3. ④

4. (1) ③

(2) ④

(3) ①

(4) ②

Lecture 2

Exercise 1

1. (1) ③

(2) ②

(3) ③

(4) ②

2. ①

3. ③

4. ②

5. (1) ①

(2) ②

(3) ③

(4) ①

(5) ③

(6) ②

6. (1) ①, ③

(2) ①, ②, ③

UNIT 5

Warm Up

QUIZ 1

1. ①

2. ②

Lecture 1

Exercise 1

1. (1) successful

(2) hesitant

(3) married

(4) dead

(5) behaved

2. (1) envious

(2) appreciative

(3) comprised

(4) suspicious

(5) resentful

3. (1) scary

(2) intriguing

(3) disturbing

(4) disruptive

(5) amazing

Lecture 2

Exercise 1

1. (1) cook

(2) eater

(3) composer

(4) occurrence

(5) speaker

2. (1) make, attempt

(2) made, plan

(3) made, promise

(4) make, appearance

3. (1) wise, decision

(2) accidental, discovery

(3) quick, amendment

UNIT 6

Warm Up

QUIZ

1. ①
2. ④
3. ①
4. ②
5. ④
6. ①

Lecture 1

Exercise 1

1. (1) on
   (2) in
   (3) in
   (4) on
   (5) in
   (6) on
   (7) on
2. (1) He, in, the, leg
   (2) She, in, the, ribs
   (3) She, in, the, eye
   (4) He, in, the, chest
   (5) The, boy, on, the, bottom
   (6) The, boy, on, the, back

Lecture 2

Exercise 1

1. (1) her, by, the, sleeve
   (2) Achilles, by(around), the, right, ankle
   (3) the, burglar, by, the, collar
   (4) his, mom, by, the, ear
   (5) him, by, the, hand
2. (1) the, suspect, around, the, wrists
   (2) the, bull, around, the, horn
   (3) Samson, around, the, legs
   (4) grabbed, each, other, around, the, waist
   (5) hugged, his, mom, around, the, neck
3. (1) a번 문장은 Jack이 그녀의 팔을 한 손으로 잡는 다는 의미이고 b번 문장은 Jack이 한 손으로 그녀의 팔을 둘러싸듯이 잡거나 두 손으로 그녀의 팔을 둘러싸듯이 잡는다는 의미이다.
   (2) a번 문장은 Achilles의 어머니가 Achilles의 발목을 한 손으로 잡는 다는 의미이고 b번 문장은 Achilles의 어머니가 Achilles의 발목을 한 손으로 둘러싸듯이 잡거나 두 손으로 둘러싸듯이 잡는다는 의미이다.

UNIT 7

Warm Up

QUIZ

1. ①, ④
2. ①, ④
3. ③

Lecture 1

Exercise 1

1. ①
2. ②
3. ③

Exercise 2

1. prefer, succeed
2. claim, failed
3. admitted, made

Exercise 3

1. (1) B
   (2) A

(3) A
(4) A
(5) B
(6) B
(7) B
(8) B
(9) A
(10) B
(11) A
(12) B
(13) A
(14) B
(15) A
(16) B
(17) A
(18) B
(19) B
(20) B
(21) A

Exercise 4

1. (1) to, share
   (2) not, having
   (3) selling
   (4) to, say
   (5) to, lock
   (6) having, been

Lecture 2

Exercise 1

1. to, be
2. to, have
3. to, lose
4. to, have, failed
5. to, have, scored
6. to, have, found

GRAMMAR DNA 총정리 연습문제 UNIT 1~7

1. ③
2. ④
3. ③
4. ④
5. ④
6. ②
7. ④
8. ① likely ② to
9. ②
10. ①
11. ① to ② see
12. ① to ② have
13. b
14. a
15. c
16. d
17. e
18. b
19. ②
20. ②
21. b
22. e
23. d
24. c
25. successful
26. suspicious, of
27. is, appreciative, of
28. made, tour, of
29. was, scary, to
30. good, cook
31. on
32. in
33. in
34. on
35. by, around
36. around

37. to, live
38. not, to
39. having
40. having, been

UNIT 9

Warm Up

QUIZ

1. ③
2. ⑤
3. ④
4. ②
5. ①

Lecture 1

Exercise 1

1. ①
2. ④
3. ②
4. ④

Exercise 2

1. ④
2. (1) When turning the corner
   (2) Since entering university
   (3) Though wearing a coat
   (4) While running for the bus
   (5) After having graduated from college
   (6) Before going to the USA
   (7) Having no money
3. ⑤, ⑥, ⑩, ⑪

Lecture 2

Exercise 1

1. 주절의 주어와 종속절의 주어가 동일하다.

Exercise 2

1. ①, ②
2. ③, ④

Exercise 3

1. ① The store opening
   ② The rain pouring
   ③ The earthquake starting
   ④ The curtains closing
   ⑤ The rooster crowing

UNIT 10

Warm Up

QUIZ

1. ②
2. ②
3. ③
4. ①
5. ④
6. ④

Lecture 1

Exercise 1

1. (1) was stolen in the robbery
   (2) has been cleaned
   (3) is being used
2. (1) was
   (2) are
   (3) being
   (4) been
   (5) be

3. (1) 진행상
   (2) 연결어
   (3) 연결어
   (4) 연결어
4. (1) ①
   (2) ①
   (3) ②
   (4) ③

Lecture 2

Exercise 1

1. (1) ③
   (2) ④
   (3) ①
2. (1) being, touched
   (2) being, treated
   (3) to, be
   (4) been, forgotten
   (5) having, been

UNIT 11

Warm Up

QUIZ

1. B형
2. A형
3. B형
4. A형
5. B형
6. A형
7. A형
8. B형
9. B형
10. B형

Lecture 1

Exercise 1

1. ②
2. ①
3. ①
4. ①
5. ②
6. ②
7. ③

Lecture 2

Exercise 1

(1) to, break up
(2) There, to, be
(3) to, be
(4) to, have, been
(5) she, to, arrive
(6) Aren't, to, admit
(7) she, to, be
(8) he, to, have, been

UNIT 12

Warm Up

QUIZ 1

1. ①
2. ③

QUIZ 2

1. ①
2. ①

QUIZ 3

1. ③
2. ③

Lecture 1

Exercise 1

1. (1) It, worries
   (2) It, is, worth
2. (1) It, is, important
   (2) It, was, not, easy
3. (1) Is, it
   (2) Does, it
4. (1) who, have, defected, from
   (2) to, unify

Lecture 2

Exercise 1

1. (1) it, clearly, understood
   (2) it, a, thought
   (3) it, useless
   (4) it, very, difficult
2. (1) who, had, flown, in
   (2) that, she, might, get, a, promotion
   (3) not, to, receive, the, prize, from, the, committee
   (4) who, had, participated
3. (1) to, London
   (2) to, Korea

UNIT 13

Warm Up

QUIZ 1

1. ④
2. ②
3. ①
4. ②

QUIZ 2

1. ④
2. ①
3. ①
4. ④

Lecture 1

Exercise 1

1. ②
2. ①

Exercise 2

1. ③
2. ④
3. ②
4. ①

Exercise 3

1. ①
2. ③
3. ③
4. ④

Lecture 2

Exercise 1

1. hasn't, yet
2. should, not
3. is, too

Exercise 2

1. don't, either
2. did, too

Exercise 3

1. didn't
2. do
3. am

4. isn't

Exercise 4

1. ①
2. ③
3. ④

UNIT 14

Warm Up

QUIZ

1. ③
2. ①, ②
3. ①

Lecture 1

Exercise 1

1. (1) Is
   (2) Are
   (3) Will
   (4) Did

Exercise 2

1. (1) Isn't
   (2) Doesn't
   (3) Don't
   (4) Won't

Exercise 3

1. (1) if, she, will
   (2) if, she, went
   (3) whether, or, not, she, will
   (4) whether, or, not, he, will
   (5) whether, or, not, she, went

Lecture 2

Exercise 1

1. (1) Which, hospital, will
   (2) Which, plastic, surgeon, will
   (3) Which, daughter, will
   (4) Which, nurse, will
2. (1) Who(Whom), did
   (2) What, did
   (3) How, much, did
   (4) Where, does, she

Exercise 3

1. (1) what, plastic, surgery, she
   (2) which, dental, clinic, she
   (3) where, she, had
   (4) how, will

Exercise 4

1. (1) Who, does
   (2) Which, daughter, does

Exercise 5

1. (1) Does, where
   (2) Do, how

GRAMMAR DNA 총정리 연습문제 UNIT 9~14

1. having, spent
2. After, having, lost
3. when, being, scolded
4. her, daughter, to, be
5. Not, having, money
6. ①, ②, ③
7. ②, ③
8. ④
9. ①

10. ①, ④

11. ①

12. ③

13. ②

14. ④

15. ⑤

16. ③

17. ④

18. ④

19. ③

20. ③

21. ②

22. ①

23. ②

24. ①

25. ①

26. It, worries

27. It, was, not

28. Does, it

29. to, unify

30. it, clearly, understood

31. has, not

32. should, not

33. is, too

34. don't, either

35. did, too

36. ②

37. ②

38. ①

39. ②

40. how, much, it, will

GRAMMAR DNA
영어 문장 분석의 새로운 패러다임

초판 인쇄 2013년 10월 8일
초판 발행 2013년 10월 15일

지은이 조기석
발행인 박 철
발행처 한국외국어대학교 출판부
130-791 서울특별시 동대문구 이문로 107
전화 02)2173-2495~7
팩스 02)2173-3363
홈페이지 http://press.hufs.ac.kr
전자우편 press@hufs.ac.kr
출판등록 제6-6호(1969. 4. 30)
디자인 · 편집 디자인퍼브 02)2254-4308
인쇄 · 제본 현문자현 031)902-1424

ISBN 978-89-7464-885-5 13740 정가 20,000원

*잘못된 책은 교환하여 드립니다.

HUINE은 한국외국어대학교출판부의 어학 및 사회과학도서 Sub Brand이다. 한국외대의 영문명인 HUFS, 현명한 국제전문가 양성의(International+Intelligent)의 의미를 담고 있으며, 휴인(携引)의 뜻인 '이끌다, 끌고 나가다'라는 의미처럼 출판계를 이끄는 리더로서, 혁신의 이미지를 담고 있다.